APPLIED NEURAL NETWORKS AND SOFT COMPUTING

APPLIED NEURAL NETWORKS AND SOFT COMPUTING

Ivan Stanimirović

ARCLER
PRESS

www.arclerpress.com

Applied Neural Networks and Soft Computing

Ivan Stanimirović

Arcler Press
2010 Winston Park Drive,
2nd Floor
Oakville, ON L6H 5R7
Canada
www.arclerpress.com
Tel: 001-289-291-7705
001-905-616-2116
Fax: 001-289-291-7601
Email: orders@arclereducation.com

ISBN: 978-1-77361-386-4 (Hardcover)

ABOUT THE AUTHOR

Ivan Stanimirović gained his PhD from University of Niš, Serbia in 2013. His work spans from multi-objective optimization methods to applications of generalized matrix inverses in areas such as image processing and computer graphics and visualisations. He is currently working as an Assistant professor at Faculty of Sciences and Mathematics at University of Niš on computing generalized matrix inverses and its applications.

TABLE OF CONTENTS

LIST OF FIGURES

LIST OF TABLES

PREFACE

When working in the field of Neural Networks, we must begin by showing a clear and obvious connection between machines and the human brain. The most important and decisive difference is the way it is produced the storage of information in the brain and the computer.

Neural Networks are a very diverse family of architectures. They are based on brain model neurons make connections between them (synapses), so that when an animal receives a stimulus, some connections are strengthened more than others, causing some response. Whenever the animal receives a stimulus (input) similar, it will generate the same response (learning): You can say that the brain recognizes different patterns.

This behavior is easily characterizable by mathematical modeling (simulation). The information processing (computer) will not be traditional: based on the temporal evolution of the system and the interpretation of certain parameters (information). The system consists of a large number of highly interconnected simple units (neurons) is massive parallelism. It can be said that a neuron is a type of PLC (dynamic system), hence the temporary. Artificial Neural Networks can learn by modifying the "weight" of connections between units; so it is possible to distinguish patterns.

The idea of Neural Networks is to define a function from which to distinguish patterns with output data: depending on the input value obtained cataloged as belonging to a certain group. The type of inputs and their number will determine the ability of net discrimination [1].

McCulloch and Pitts conducted in 1943 a biological study of the brain obtaining a formal model of a neuron, which thus introduced the concept of the threshold: a neuron responds to a stimulus provided it exceeds a certain threshold.

Later, in 1949, Hebb developed the Hebbian Learning: learning by adapting synapses or strengthening of connections. In 1959, Rosenblat defined the Perceptron, one of the most important in the development of Neural Networks concepts: Perceptron is a learning rule or rule perceptron structure. This structure is the combination of a neuron and an output function that is defining the threshold. Neuron mission is to implement a linear combination of the inputs. Each entry has a weight temporarily adapted. This is what is known as learning.

Misky and Papert developed in 1969 a single perceptron getting rated first order (XOR). The problem of training several layers are then raised. Thus in 1974 Werbos defined the backpropagation algorithm and the use of the sigmoid function as an output function perceptron. The backpropagation algorithm to modify the weights based on the last layer to the starting based on the error in the previous iteration. That error is the difference between the output of the Neural Network and the actual output we should have obtained. As the backpropagation algorithm is based on the derivative of the error, it was decided to use the sigmoid function instead of the step to represent the activation threshold (the step function has an infinite derivative at the origin).

Later other types of networks were developed: Kohonen in the 70s created the topological maps and associative memories, and in 1982 defined Hopfield Hopfield networks.

Finally, Rumelhart and McClelland in 1986 developed the multilayer perceptron, and popularized the backpropagation algorithm. In 1989, Cybenko, Hornik et al. and the multilayer perceptron Funahashi defined as a universal approximator [1].

This book investigates potential applications of Neural Networks, where the behavior is easily characterizable by mathematical modeling (simulation). The information processing (computer) will not be traditional: based on the temporal evolution of the system and the interpretation of certain parameters (information). The system consists of a large number of highly interconnected simple units (neurons) is massive parallelism. It can be said that a neuron is a type of PLC (dynamic system), hence the temporary. Artificial Neural Networks can learn by modifying the "weight" of connections between units; so it is possible to distinguish patterns.

The idea of Neural Networks will be considered in order to define a function from which to distinguish patterns with output data: depending on the input value obtained cataloged as belonging to a certain group. The type of inputs and their number will determine the ability of net discrimination.

1
CHAPTER

INTRODUCTION

CONTENTS

There are different classification criteria for Neural Networks:

- Temporal characterization: It refers to the temporal characterization of entries.
- Continuous in time: when the input function is a continuous function. Such networks are used in systems where the immediate classification of inputs, such as an alarm system that is activated in the presence of certain hazardous parameters is necessary.
- NOW: when entries are taken at certain time points. They are used in systems that do not require immediate control of the entries and only seeks its evolution without saturating the system too with lots of data.
- Entry: It refers to the values that make the entries.
- Binary: zero or one. It can be used when the inputs are encoded, for example, representing the interval over which fall within a range. If the range is divided into x intervals, each entry is represented by x values, all but one to zero, which corresponds to the interval of input values.
- Keep going: the input value can be anywhere within a range. You can define different ranges of variation.
- Training: It refers to learning followed by Network.
- Supervised: when the evolution of the network is monitored. For example, when you are offered to the Red examples pointing out the outputs should be obtained.
- With reward/punishment: When the network succeeds is offered a reward. When failure is punished. So learn how to behave.
- Unsupervised: It is not told Network what to give. This is often used in cases where we have a number of inputs and do not know how to classify them. Depending on what we get after training a classification.
- Feedforward: feedback forward. It is the normal structure where the outputs of a layer are introduced in the following.
- Feedback: feedback back. The outputs of certain layers are introduced in previous layers so that they know what has been the subsequent behavior and adapt accordingly.
- Among the most representative models are associative maps, the multilayer perceptron, Hopfield networks (auto-associative

memories), the self-organizing Kohonen topological maps and networks hebbianas [Martín-01].

In the Figure 1.1, an input (x1) is not sufficient to determine whether we are in the pattern A or B. In another entry (x2) we are already able to discriminate.

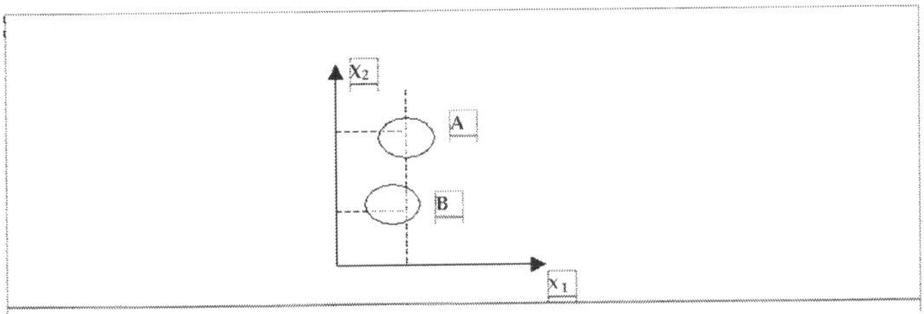

Figure 1.1. Example of classification, (*Source: self-made or CC-BY license*).

1. Characterization of Neuronal Network

The three key points to develop a Neuronal Network are:

- Characterization of the neuron (basic unit of computing);
- Defining an interconnection topology; and
- Definition of learning rules.

2. Properties of Neuronal Network

The properties shared by all Neural Networks are:

- High degree of parallelism: multiple neurons may be working at a time.
- Easy Deployment Hardware (or software).
- Robustness against possible failures: the information is distributed.
- Adaptive nature that sustains learning ability.
- Generalizability: from a ticket, we define a pattern.

On the computer, the data stored in positions memory cells that are isolated from each other. So when you want to access a position memory the data of this cell is obtained, without the positions of memory Adjoining are affected by the operation.

In the brain, management it's totally different. When we look for information you do not need to know where it is stored and actually, we cannot know because nobody knows where you keep the brain the data.

Worldwide but especially in U.S. and Japan, experts scientists try to find the key the memory associative. If you got to build a chip memory according to the human model, the science give a giant step in the fascinating race to the artificial intelligence.

Human brain is a system process multi-purpose data capable of treating large number of very different information and in no time and with the highest practical sense to immediately power act accordingly.

Computers in change are highly specialized with capacity to process information accurately very specific (in principle only numbers) following instructions given.

The human brain has more than ten million neurons, which are already present at birth. As time passes some of them may become inactive. Our body thought consumes energy biochemistry the equivalent of a tablespoon of sugar per hour. Home computers consume a similar amount.

According to specialized studies, the brain has two mechanisms storage of data: the memory intermediate accepts five to ten units of information, but only keeps for a few minutes. The memory ultimately keeps the information "for life," which does not mean that we can always agree on everything. The memory immediate works as a kind of continuous tape: information circulates rotatively form of electrical impulses by records.

Thus, the system is comparable to the memory of a dynamic computer, in which information has to be continually refreshed so you do not miss out. In change, the final memory seems rather to resemble known memory of computers. It is believed that this memory is powered by chemical formations proteins present in the human brain.

1.1. DIFFERENCES BETWEEN THE BRAIN AND A COMPUTER

We can summarize the main differences between the brain and a computer in the Table 1.1.

Table 1.1. Main differences between the brain and a computer

Brain	**Computer**
Data system capable of handling multi-purpose large amount of information in a short time but not necessarily accurately.	Highly specialized systems capable of processing very specific information, following instructions given.

The frequency of nerve impulses can vary.	The transmission frequency is unchanged and is given by the internal clock of the machine.
Called synapses in the brain meets the simultaneous function of several gates (AND, OR, NOT, etc.)	The logic gates have a perfectly determined and unalterable function.
Memory is the associative and do not know where will be stored.	The information is stored in memory locations shortcut for their address.
The impulses flow 30 meters per second.	Inside a computer, pulses flow the speed of the light.

1.1.1. Similarities between the Brain and a Computer

- Both encode information into digital pulses.
- Both the brain and computer have logic gates.
- Different types of memory.
- Both have approximately the same consumption energy.

In conclusion of the similarities and differences between machine and brain, while observing carefully the analysis above figure, we have to note that, despite the similarities between the two models, and the utility computing model RRNN, the human brain it is, today, irreplaceable. This does not mean that the usefulness of Neural Networks is, much less scarce.

1.1.2. Biologically Inspired Neural Networks

Our study model, Neural Networks, have an obvious and marked biological origin.

Broadly speaking, remember that the human brain consists of tens of trillions of neurons interconnected together to form circuits or networks that carry out specific functions.

A typical neuron collects signals from other neurons through a plethora of delicate structures called dendrites. The neuron emits pulses of electrical activity along a long thin fiber called an axon, which cleaves in thousands of branches.

We can see in the Figure 1.2 the structure of a neuron.

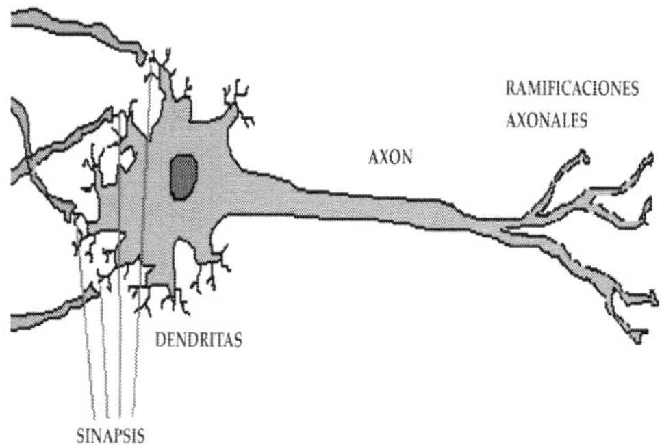

Figure 1.2. The structure of a human neuron, (*Source: self-made or CC-BY license*).

The ends of these branches reach to the dendrites of other neurons called synapses and establish a connection, in which an electrical impulse transformation into a neurochemical message occurs, by releasing substances called neurotransmitters.

The effect of neurotransmitters on the receiving neuron excitatory or inhibitory can be, and is variable (the intensity of the effect depends on numerous factors that would not be appropriate to describe here) so we can talk about the strength or effectiveness of a synapse. Excitatory and inhibitory signals received by a neuron are combined, and depending on total stimulation received, the neuron takes a certain level of activation, which results in the generation of short nerve impulses at a certain frequency or firing rate, and its propagation along the axon to the neurons which "connects" (Figure 1.3).

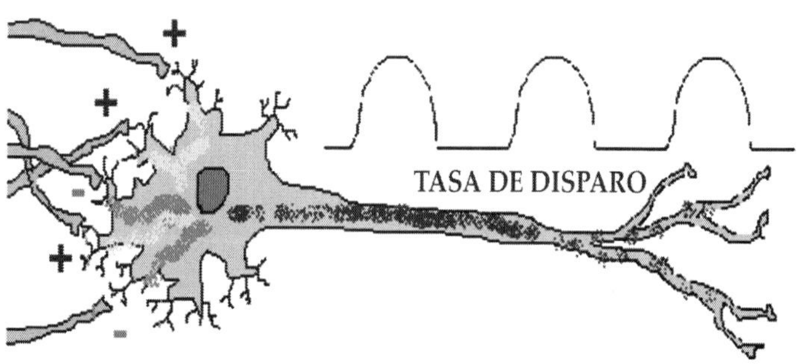

Figure 1.3. The frequency of the neural impulses, (*Source: self-made or CC-BY license*).

In this way, information is transmitted from a neuron to another and will be processed through synaptic connections and the neurons themselves. Learning Neural Networks is produced by varying the effectiveness of synapses, thus changing the influence of some neurons exert on others, hence it follows that architecture, the type, and effectiveness of the connections at a time given represent memory somehow or state of knowledge of the network.

1.2. ARTIFICIAL NEURAL NETWORKS

Neurons are modeled by processing units. Each processing unit comprises a network of input connections, a network function (propagation), responsible for computing the total combined input of all connections, a central processing core, responsible for implementing the activation function, and exit, where the trigger value is transmitted to other units.

The Table 1.2 can illustrate the similarities between the artificial neurons and biological neurons:

Table 1.2. Similarities between the artificial neurons and biological neurons

Biological Neural Networks	***Artificial Neural Networks***
Neurons	Processing units
Synaptic connections	Weighted connections
Effectiveness of synapses	Weight of connections
Excitatory or inhibitory effect of a connection	Sign of a connection weight
Combined effect of synapses	Propagation function or network
Activation -> firing rate	Activation function -> Output

During the 1990s, ANNs began to be applied to different fields of knowledge: classification robotics, artificial vision, signal processing, writing and speech recognition, and so on. In this in this context, documentary applications have not been able to remain outside this process.

1.3. DEFINITION AND CHARACTERISTICS

ANN can be characterized as a data handling framework made out of an extensive number of preparing components (neurons), abundantly associated with each other through correspondence channels (Reguero, 1995). These associations build up a progressive structure and permit the connection with objects of this present reality endeavoring to copy the organic sensory system. Not at all like processing in view of unsurprising calculations, neural calculation permits take care of complex issues whose scientific formalization is amazingly troublesome. This is accomplished because of the standards of ANN working, of which we refer to underneath the five most imperative (Row, 1995).

Adaptive taking in: this is maybe the most imperative element of ANN, since they can carry on in light of a preparation with a progression of illustrative cases. Along these lines, no it is important to expand a from the earlier model, or to set up probabilistic capacities. An ANN is versatile on the grounds that it can be continually altered keeping in mind the end goal to adjust to new states of work.

Self-association: while learning is where the inside data of the ANN, self-association comprises of changing the whole total system with a specific end goal to complete a particular target. Self-association implies speculation, so a system can react to information or circumstances that you have not experienced previously, but rather which you can deduce in light of your preparation. This element is extremely helpful particularly when the info data is indistinct or is fragmented.

Fault Tolerance: In conventional processing, the departure of a little snippet of data can ordinarily prompt framework disablement. ANNs have a high limit of resilience to disappointments. Adaptation to non-critical failure is comprehended here in two detects: to begin with, systems can perceive data designs with commotion, mutilation or deficiency (adaptation to non-critical failure as for of the information). Furthermore, they can keep working (with some corruption) regardless of whether it is wrecked piece of the system (adaptation to non-critical failure as for the structure). While customary processing stores data in one of a kind, limited spaces, and addressable, neural systems do as such in an appropriated and high level of repetition.

Real-time task: of every current technique, ANN are the most appropriate for the acknowledgment of examples continuously, in light of the fact that they work in parallel refreshing every one of their occasions at the same time. Note that this component is just refreshing when actualized systems with equipment exceptionally intended for parallel handling.

Easy inclusion in existing innovation: it is generally simple to acquire particular chips for systems that enhance your capacity in specific undertakings. This encourages particular joining in frameworks existing ones.

ANNs are data preparing models in light of the working of the human mind. They are shaped by countless or preparing components called neurons, which we can partition into three unique gatherings: (1) those that get data from outside, likewise called as info neurons; (2) those that transmit data to the outside, designated neurons lastly the individuals who have no contact with the outside and 48 with different neurons in the system, these are called concealed neurons. In an ANN neurons are unequivocally interconnected with each other, composed in layers and shaping distinctive topologies. There are distinctive topologies to take care of various kinds of issues.

In Figure 1.4, we can see a schematic diagram of a neuron (Regueiro, 1995). It has a variable quantity of inputs $(Xo,\ldots,.X_{Q+M})$ that come from the outside (in the event that our neuron is in the info layer of the system), or different neurons (on the off chance that it is in some concealed layer or yield). Thusly it has a solitary yield (X) that will transmit the data to the outside (on the off chance that our neuron is in the yield layer of the system), or towards different neurons (in the event that it is in the layer of passage or in some hid). The yield flag will be figured by the contributions, for which every last one of them is influenced by a specific weight. These weights fluctuate openly as an element of time and in every one of the neurons that are a piece of the system, and this is critical in light of the fact that the information that contains the system will be in said weights. All info signals are consolidated by called joining capacity (fj), which may shift as indicated by the sort of neuron yet will dependably create a vector whose segments will decide the last yield an incentive by the actuation work (g). Also, there are diverse sorts of actuation works, the most widely recognized are step work, direct or blended capacity, sigmoidal, and Gaussian capacity. Each capacity has its own particular qualities, and will be utilized by the kind of data that we will oversee (e.g., parallel or simple, and so forth).

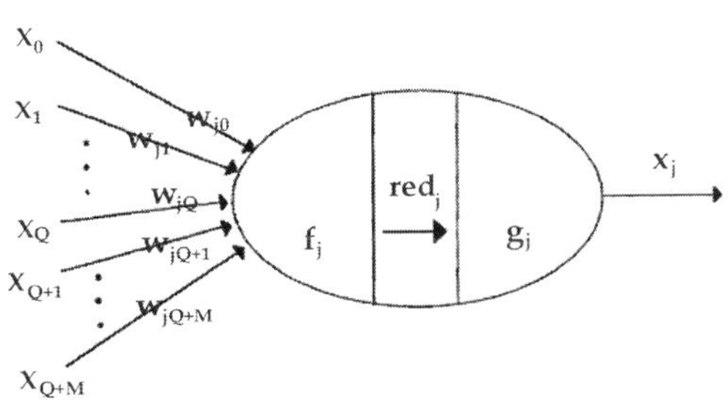

Figure 1.4. A schematic diagram of a neuron, (*Source: self-made or CC-BY license*).

As we have officially expressed, as in the human sensory system, information is found in the weights of associations amongst neurons, and not in the neurons themselves. These weights have no consistent esteem, however which fluctuate contingent upon a specific calculation called learning guideline. An administer of learning influences the estimation of the weights of a system to fluctuate until the point when they embrace a consistent esteem, when this happens it is said that the system has effectively "learned." There are wide ranges of learning rules, yet we could part them in two huge gatherings: (i) those of directed learning, and (ii) those of unsupervised learning. In the in the first place, there is an example of data that fills in for instance for the system to learn, while in the last does not exist this data and the weights of the system vacillate openly with no sort of reference, until the point that they balance out.

Inside every one of these two gatherings, there are a few calculations that we won't name here and which are related with various system models. At long last we can state that there is another standard of arrangement of learning rules, which is identified with the type of activity of the direction: (i) disconnected, and (ii) connected. In the primary case, the system must be disengaged from its task until the point when the learning closes, to then set its weights and begin working. In the second case, learning happens amid the typical task of the system, so that here the learning period of the activity isn't extraordinary. The primary distinction between the two will be in disconnected systems will be more steady in their task than online.

We have just perceived how this compound is a preparing component or neuron (microstructure). Associating a few neurons absolutely we get a system (meso-structure). There are limitless varieties of topologies, however, we can characterize them as indicated by four criteria: (i) number of levels or layers, (ii) number of neurons per level, and (iii) types of association.

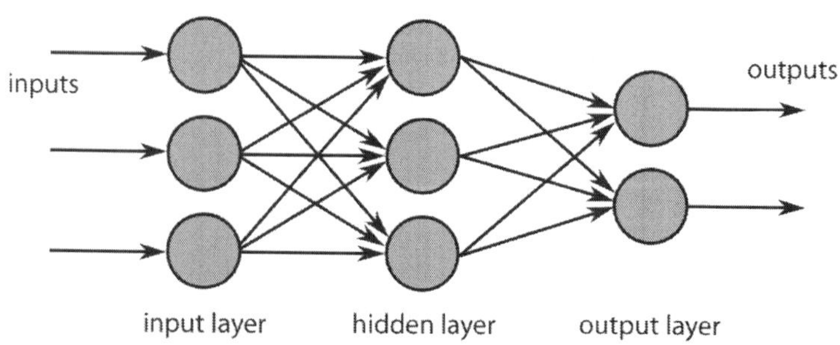

Figure 1.5. Neural Network with multiple layers, (*Source: self-made or CC-BY license*).

In level of entry levels hidden level of departure as for the number of layers, we can say that a network can be formed by a minimum of one layer and a maximum of n layers. When there is only one layer, this officiates both inbound and outbound. In the case of a two-layer network, the first will be input and the second output. In the case of networks with more than three layers, as the one of Figure 1.2, the first one will be of entrance, the last of exit and the rest will be the layers hidden as we mentioned above. The number of neurons per level can vary from 1 to n, and depends of the topology of each particular model.

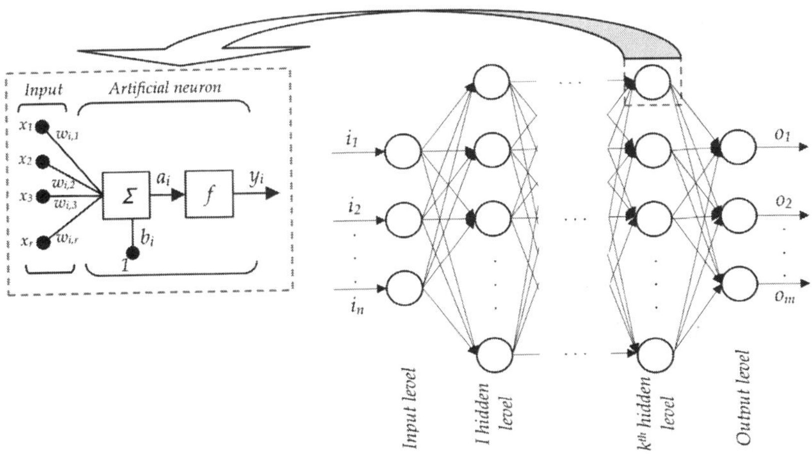

Figure 1.6. Neural Network with feedback of the outputs to the previous inputs or to the neurons of the same level, (*Source: self-made or CC-BY license*).

The manner by which the yield of a specific layer of neurons is associated with the contribution of another decides the availability of the system. Here are two essential structures:

1) When no yield from a layer is contribution of a similar level or of past levels, called forward spread (Figure 1.5),
2) When there is some sort of criticism of the yields to the past sources of info or of a similar level, designated engendering to the back (Figure 1.6). Every one of the highlights recorded does not state excessively without anyone else, so it should the system demonstrate that embraces it, nonetheless, such an examination goes past the goals of this article.

As we have rehashed all through the work, there are a few unique models of neural systems. Every one of them has been intended for pretty much particular purposes, be that as it may, there are a few who have won awesome notoriety.

1.3.1. The Kohonen Model

Before entering completely into the uses of ANN in the field of Documentation we will stop quickly to examine one of the models of the past table most utilized as a part of data recovery, is the one created by Teuvo Kohonen. Toward the start of the 1980s, Kohonen demonstrated that data without anyone else, expecting its own particular structure and a practical depiction of the conduct of the system, was adequate to constrain the arrangement of topological maps (Kohonen, 1982). These maps have the element of arranging the info data via naturally arranging it.

This model has two variations:

1) The purported "Vector Quantification of Learning" (Learning Vector Quantization) or LVQ.
2) The purported "Topology-Preserving Map" or TPM. The last is likewise regularly alluded to as a "Self-Organizing Map" (SOM). The distinction between the two models is that while the LVQ works with yields in a solitary measurement, the yield in the SOM is two-dimensional. The last is the most across the board.

The rule of task of this model is straightforward, it involves setting up a correspondence between the info data and a two-dimensional yield space, or topological guide. Along these lines, the info information with normal highlights will initiate regions close to the guide. It is exceptionally normal to speak to this system show with its yield neurons masterminded in a two-dimensional manner, as should be obvious in Figure 1.4. At the point when an information is gone into the system, it responds such that exclusive a neuron of the layer of yield is initiated. This neuron is known as the victor take-all unit and decides a point on the two-dimensional guide. What the system is truly doing is arranging the info data, since the triumphant neuron speaks to the class to which the information has a place, notwithstanding that before comparative sources of info a similar neuron will dependably be enacted. Along these lines, the system is profoundly demonstrated to build up relations, obscure beforehand, between a specific arrangement of information.

SOM display with its yield neurons framing the guide the learning technique for the SOM show is called aggressive and is of the unsupervised and disconnected write, so it will have a past phase of preparing and a later phase of task. The Kohonen show is a standout amongst the most helpful ANNs that have been produced, in spite of the fact that it has two restrictions: 1) the way toward learning is frequently long and challenging, and 2) to learn new information it is important to rehash the learning procedure totally. Be that as it may, the flexibility of this kind of system is exceptionally expansive, enabling you to order all sort of data, from scholarly (Honkela, 1995) to monetary (Kaski, 1995). Later they will be seen distinctive uses of this model.

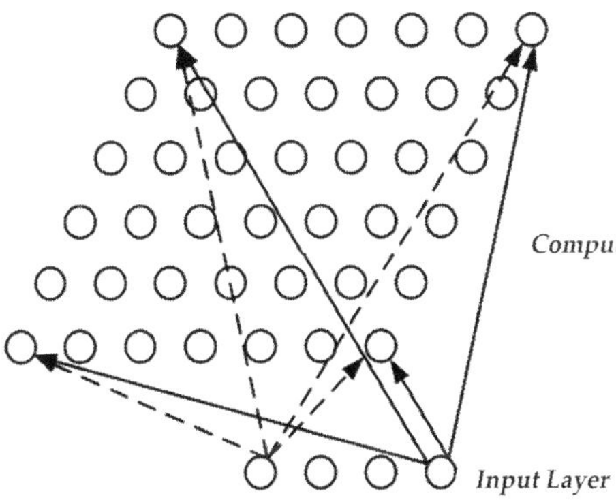

Figure 1.7. Network model with its output neurons arranged in a two-dimensional way, (Source: self-made or CC-BY license).

The network function is typically the weighted summation, whereas the activation function is typically a threshold function or a sigmoidal function.

Let's see in detail each of the terms listed here:

Propagation function or network: Calculate the baseline value or total input to the unit, generally as a simple weighted sum of all entries received, i.e., the inputs multiplied by the weight or value of connections. Equivalent to the combination of excitatory and inhibitory signals of biological neurons.

1.3.2. Linear Function of Base (LBF)

It consists of the sum of the weighted inputs. It is a hyperplane function type, i.e., first order.

Given a unit j, and n units connected to it, if we call X the input vector (which coincides with the outputs of the units of the previous layer) and the weight vector Wj of the corresponding connections, this function would look like:

$$net_j\left(X,W_j\right)=\sum_{i=1}^{n}x_i w_{ij}$$

By representing the weights used two subscripts to indicate that connect two units, i and j, where j refers drive current.

1.3.3. Radial Basis Function (RBF)

Nonlinear function hyperspherical type second order. The net value represents the distance to a particular reference pattern.

$$net_j\left(X,W_j\right)=\sqrt{\sum_{i=1}^{n}(x_i-w_{ij})^2}$$

1.3.3.1. Activation Function

It is perhaps the primary or defining characteristic of neurons, which better defines the behavior of the same. Different types of functions are used, from simple single-function threshold nonlinear functions. It is responsible for calculating the level or state of the neuron activation function of the total input.

Usually, it distinguishes between linear functions, in which the output is proportional to the input; threshold functions in which the output is a (typically binary 0/1) discrete value that depends on if the total stimulation exceeds or not a certain threshold value; nonlinear functions, not proportional to the input.

1.3.3.2. Threshold Function

Initially it was thought that the neurons used a threshold function, i.e., that were inactive and activated only if the total stimulation exceeded a certain limit value. This can be modeled by a step function: the most typical is the unit step: the function returns 0 below the critical value (threshold) and one above.

After it was found that neurons emitted pulses of electrical activity with a variable frequency, depending on the intensity of stimulation received, and had some activity even at rest, with no stimulation. These findings led to the use of non-linear functions with those characteristics, as the sigmoid function, a step similar to a threshold function profile, but continuous.

1.3.3.3. Sigmoidal Function or Logistics

It is probably the most used activation function today.

$$act_j\left(net\right)=\frac{1}{1+e^{-net_j i\sigma}}$$

It is a non-linear continuous function quite physiological plausibility.

The sigmoidal function has a range between 0 and 1. This applied to the processing units of an artificial Neural Network means that, regardless of the input, the output will be between 0 and 1.

This function depends on the parameter s, which usually takes the value 1.

We can observe the graphical representation of the latter in the following graph:

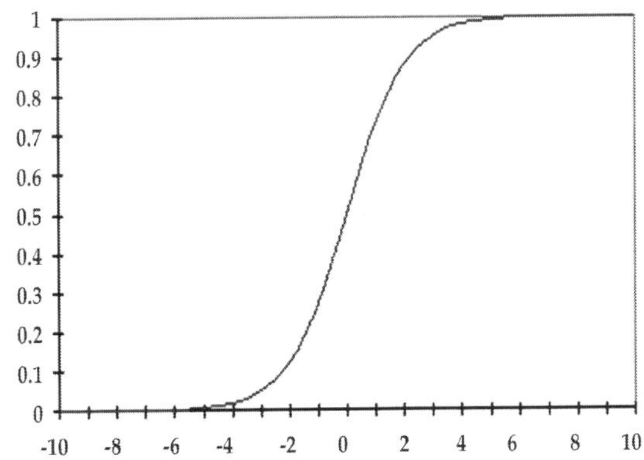

The output unit is 0.5 when the input is zero, this means that the unit has some activity even in the absence of stimulation. By increasing the stimulation unit increases its activation, and decreases if stimulation is inhibitory, as similarly to real neurons behave.

It has the following desirable features:

- Accommodating very strong signals without producing saturation.
- Supports weak signals without excessive attenuation.
- Easily derivable, since.

$$f'(x) = f(x)(1 - f(x))dx$$

The main limitation of this feature is that it serves to express polarities, always it gives positive values. An alternative function with similar qualities but with a range between –1 and 1 is the hyperbolic tangent function. From a physiological point of view, the negative sign can be interpreted as a decrease in the firing rate of a neuron below the firing rate at rest.

1.3.3.4. Gaussian Function

$$act_j(net) = ce^{-net_j i\sigma}$$

Weighted connections: Play the role of synaptic connections, the weight of the connection equals strength or effectiveness of the synapse. The existence of connection determines whether a unit may influence over another, the value of the weights and the sign thereof define the type (excitatory/inhibitory) and the intensity of the influence.

Departure: Calculates the output of the neuron activation function the same, but usually does not apply more than the identity function, and output is taken as the trigger value. The output value would fulfill the function of the firing rate in biological neurons.

1.3.4. Neural Network Architectures

To design a network must be set as units will be connected to each other and properly determine the weights of the connections. Most commonly available units in layers, it being possible to networks one, two or more than two layers, the so-called multilayer networks.

Although initially networks single layer were developed, the most common is to have three or more layers: the first layer acts as the input buffer, storing the raw data supplied to the network or performing a simple pre-process the same, the call input layer; another layer acts as an interface or output buffer, storing the network response for that can be read, the call output layer; and the intermediate layers are mainly responsible to extract, process and store information, call hidden layers (Figure 1.8).

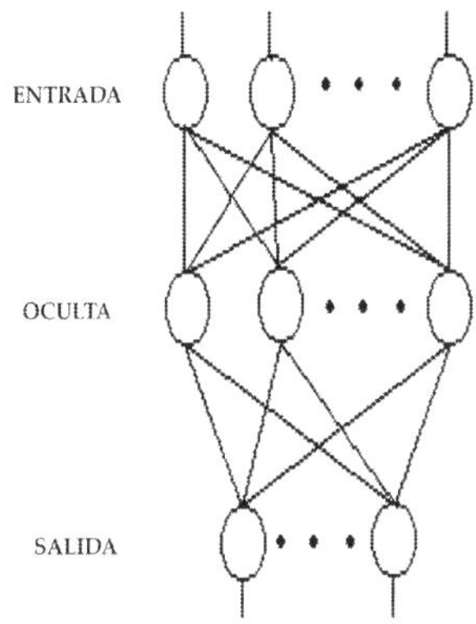

Figure 1.8. Hidden layers in the ANN, (*Source: self-made or CC-BY license*).

Besides the number of layers of a network, depending on how other layers are interconnected, we can speak of recurrent networks (feedback) and non-recurring networks or cascading (feed-forward).

In networks cascaded information flows unidirectionally from one layer to another (from the input layer to the hidden and from these to the output layer layers), and also not inter-connections allowed.

In recurrent networks information can return to places they had passed, forming loops, and intracapa connections (side) are supported, including a unit with itself.

Connections between one layer and another may be total, that is, each unit is connected to all units of the following, or partial layer, in which a unit is connected to only some of the layers of the next unit, generally following a pseudo-random (for example, using genetic algorithms) or random pattern.

1.4. PROCESSING STAGES

1.4.1. Learning Phase

Learning is presenting patterns to the network, and the subsequent modification of the weights of the connections following some learning rule that tries to optimize its response, usually by minimizing the error or optimization of any "energy function."

The simplest mode of learning is the presentation of input patterns with output patterns desired (targets) for each input pattern, so-called supervised learning. If you are not presented to the network desired output patterns, we will say that it is unsupervised learning. Because it not tells the network that results should give, but is allowed to follow some rule of self-organization. A third type of learning, halfway between the previous ones, is called reinforced learning. In this case, the supervisor merely indicates whether the output offered by the network is correct or incorrect, but does not indicate that response should be given.

Whatever the type of learning used, an essential feature of the network is the rule used learning, which indicates how the connection weights based on the data used in the input, i.e., the learning history are modified of the network. For example, between supervised learning algorithms, the generalized delta rule, Changes weights in each cycle by performing learning the increased proportional to the rate of change of the error weight by weight, in the negative.

Learning requires repeated presentation of a relatively large number of training examples until a satisfactory response system (as measured error or function of energy used).

It is usual to have a set of data other than those used for training, for which the correct answer is known, and used as a test, evaluating thus whether the network responds appropriately against data other than those used during learning (generalization), if so it is considered that the network works well and can move on to the implementation phase (recall), i.e., it can be used to get a result against completely new data for which the correct answer is not known.

1.4.2. Supervised Learning

We know that in supervised learning network presented a series of input patterns with desired output patterns. Learning involves modifying the connection weights in the direction to reduce the discrepancy between the obtained and desired output. The general steps for this algorithm are:

- Randomizing the weights of all the connections (preferably with small values).
- Select a couple of training, i.e., an input pattern and the pattern corresponding desired output (target).
- Present the input pattern and calculate the network output through the usual operations: sum of weighted inputs, activation function and transfer to the next layer, to reach the output layer. (Initially, we get random outputs, as the connection weights are random).

- Calculation error or discrepancy between the output obtained and desired. The error (objective function) is often defined as the sum of the squares of the differences between the obtained actual and desired outputs, averaged for all output units and all training patterns. If the error is less than certain criteria set in advance, increasing the number of good examples; If all examples are classified correctly, the end, but continue.
- Apply the rule learning, i.e., adjust the weights of the connections trying to reduce the error, usually by calculating rates of change or error gradients, so we talk about learning rules by descending gradient. To reduce the error will have to change the connection weights, in proportion to the relative rate of change of error with respect to weight variation, i.e., the derivative of the error on the weight, EP (error on the weight). One way to calculate the EP be slightly perturb a weight and watch the error varies, but would be inefficient if we work with many connections (this is the basis of some statistical methods discussed in another section). Later we will see a mathematical algorithm to calculate EP.
- Back to step 2.

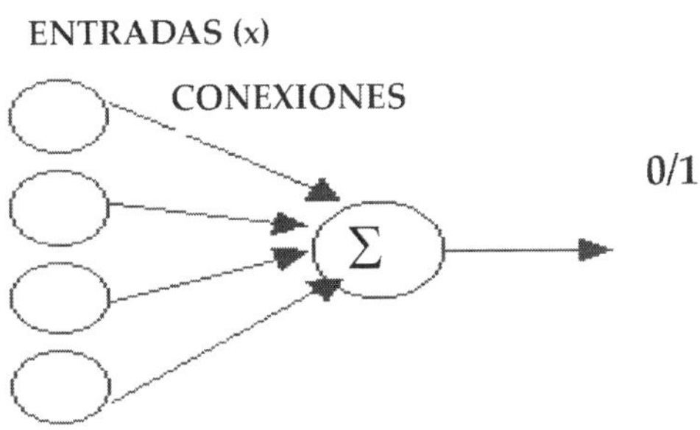

1.4.3. Unsupervised Learning

One of the main criticisms of supervised learning, leaving aside the computational aspects was its dubious biological plausibility, because:

- Propagate requires certain information (the mistake) backward, contrary to the natural flow of information. Obviously, this does not happen in real neurons, however, this objection is superficial if we consider that the brain is rich in networks retrograde one layer to another, and could use these paths in many ways to provide information supervised learning type required.

- It requires an instructor that provides the desired output. People learn to understand sentences or visual scenes without explicit instructions to do so, you could say that the brain has a mechanism of self-organization. When they presented to the network a large collection of data without telling you what to do with them, is apparently not knowing what to do. However, researchers have designed several unsupervised learning procedures, which are able to extract enough information inductively these data to enable recovery later, these algorithms are used in clustering and classification tasks.
- In unsupervised learning, it is not required to present desired output patterns. However, the algorithm and the change rule connections produce consistent output vectors, i.e., presenting a learned or like pattern, always produces the same output. It is considered that the learning process is able to extract certain statistical properties of the examples of learning and grouped into categories or classes of similar patterns.
- We do not know a priori which output corresponds to each type or group of input patterns, or what used to classify attributes, so they are very useful as generators categories (clustering)
- In general, supervised learning methods do not appeal to some notion of the quality of representation. Quality performances are characterized by economy of representation (coding cost plus the cost of reconstruction), without losing the ability to reconstruct the stored information.

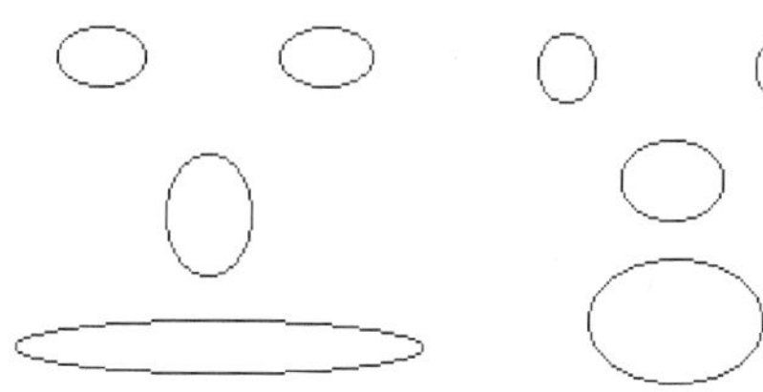

Imagine for example, images formed by ellipses, as the faces of the figure, we can represent them by bitmaps, but are possible with more efficient representations; an ellipse can be distinguished from another five attributes: orientation, vertical position, horizontal position, length and width, and therefore the image may be described using only five parameters ellipse.

There are several simple ways to find budget codes at the same time allow a good reconstruction of the entrance: main components learning, competitive learning, and demographic codes.

1.4.4. Learning Main Components

The learning involves extracting main components and describe the components of variation shared by many input units being sufficient one unit for each main component. Can be achieved by networks on a rebuild input-output units, applying backpropagation. This learning is unsupervised because since the output is the same as the input, no instructor is needed. Another way to do this without using backpropagation is based on changing the connections based on correlations between the activities of the hidden units and input units.

1.4.5. Competitive Learning

Learning by major components, a small number of units cooperating in the representation of the input pattern. In competitive learning, a large number of hidden unit's odds with one another, which finally one hidden unit is used to represent a given input pattern or a set of similar patterns? The unit selected is one whose hidden weights are more similar incidents to the input pattern. Learning is to enhance the winning unit connections and weaken each other so that the winning unit weights increasingly resemble the input pattern. Based on Hebb rule product rule or rules they are generally used. Reconstruction of the input pattern will be to copy the weight distribution of the winning unit.

1.4.6. Demographic Codes

The problem of the main components is that removes all redundancy, and thus lose fault tolerance, since each pattern or group of patterns similar entry is represented by a single neuron. The solution to this dilemma also appears to be used by the brain, are the demographic codes, a compromise between pure and distributed representations purely local representations.

This is to represent each input pattern of a set or population of simultaneously active units so that some unit dysfunction not causes loss of information.

Demographic codes seem to contradict the principle of economy of representations, however, a population of neurons is very easy to represent itself it consists of a group of neighboring neurons with a prominent center of activity. In that case, it is sufficient to describe the center, plus some measure of how the activity of adjacent units decays as the center moves away.

1.4.7. Reinforced Learning

As we discussed, the idea is similar to that of supervised learning, only here the information given by the teacher is minimal, merely to indicate whether the network response is correct or incorrect. In this sense, it is similar to the notion taken of behavioral psychology conditioning reinforcement, in summary, claims that are learned (in the sense that are more likely to be repeated) reinforced positively behaviors and vice versa (the battered behaviors or negatively reinforced reduce the possibility of appearing).

A notion closely linked to the reinforcement learning is based networks Decision. They are networks for pattern classification, similar to the idolaters pattern in which the teacher, rather than stating the exact desired output (target) indicates just the right class for each input pattern.

In networks based on the decision a discriminant function is used to determine which category or class belongs the input pattern, whether, during training, a response does not match the one given by the teacher, the weights are changed, if not leave like (hence comes the name DBNN). Learning is finding weights that give the correct classification.

1.5. TRAINING OR LEARNING

Learning involves setting interconnection weights between neurons. There are different criteria for setting:

1. Supervised:
- Heuristic: Perceptron.
- Minimizes cost function (traditional adaptive algorithms): the error function evaluation is minimized to adjust the weights. An example is the multilayer perceptron.
2. By reinforcement (with reward/penalty):
    - Actor/critic.
    - *Q-learning.*
3. Unsupervised:
- Hebbian: Hopfield.

- Competitive: Kohonen topological maps.
- Boltzmann machines.

Learning is an algorithm by which you are given data to the neuron and it learns to recognize patterns with them. Supervised learning is not the one where you have a set pattern but are not cataloged. The goal is to be the network that classify them according to criteria that are provided (similarities must meet patterns belong to a class) and as possible analogies that can be found in the input data. Supervised learning is one in which it has cataloged patterns exemplifying Network.

1.5.1. The Multilayer Perceptron

Such networks are characterized by their ease of implementation. Learning is based on the backpropagation: it is part of some initial weights in inter-neuron connections. A set of entries for a certain output is obtained. Based on the output we should have obtained (cataloged pattern – supervised learning) is known, we calculate the error. From this error, weights are modified in reverse direction to the evolution of the network (it is part of the output to reach the entrance). In the same way, it works with the rest of training inputs. It can be seen that the error will decrease as the algorithm is applied.

However, training repeated with the same entries eventually leads overtraining the Neural Network, memorizing characteristics of a set, thereby preventing learn to generalize. So after each iteration must be evaluated: enter new values other than training and calculate the output error. Thus a function (error evaluation) from which we want to find its absolute minimum (maybe local minimum) is obtained. Determining the number of iterations is reached that value, we ensure, in a way, get a lower error for any set of input data. Then you can apply a test with a new set of inputs that will give us a measure of the ability of net discrimination.

What is a perception?

A perceptron is a neural structure plus a learning rule. As explained above, a neuron is composed of a set of inputs, each with a weight, which are introduced into the body thereof for processing. Such processing may include:

1. Linear combination:

$$y=\sum_i \omega_i x_i - \theta$$

2. Euclidean distance:

$$y = \sqrt{\sum_i (w_i x_i)^2 - \theta}$$

This result is subsequently introduced into one characterized by a block of the following functions (Figure 1.9):

	Funcion	Rango	Grafica
Identidad	$y = x$	$[-\infty, +\infty]$	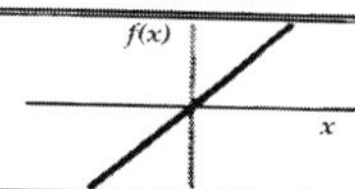
Escalon	$y = \text{sign}(x)$ $y = H(x)$	$\{-1, +1\}$ $\{0, +1\}$	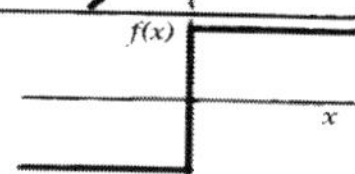
Lineal a tramos	$y = \begin{cases} -1, \text{ si } x < -1 \\ x, \text{ si } +1 \leq x \leq -1 \\ +1, \text{ si } x > +1 \end{cases}$	$[-1, +1]$	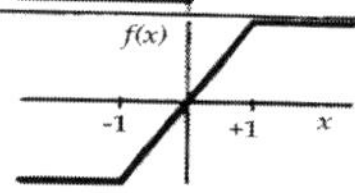
Sigmoidea	$y = \frac{1}{1 + e^{-x}}$ $y = \text{tgh}(x)$	$[0, +1]$ $[-1, +1]$	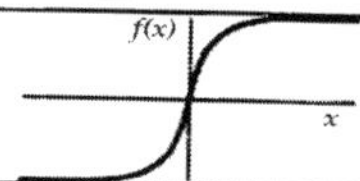
Gaussiana	$y = Ae^{-Bx^2}$	$[0, +1]$	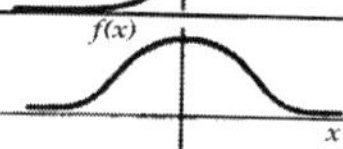
Sinusoidal	$y = A \text{ sen } (\omega x + \varphi)$	$[-1, +1]$	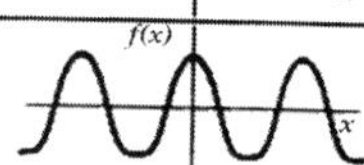

Figure 1.9. Table of possible output functions perceptron, (Source: self-made or CC-BY license).

The function representing the ideal behavior of a neuron is the step function: depending on the connection between neurons input (output = 1) or not (output = 0) is activated. This decision may depend on a threshold (the output is able to overcome it), represented in the above expressions by q: introducing this negative term is equivalent to considering that the function applies one from qy not from zero as shown in the table.

Although this is the ideal behavior in practice is often used sigmoid function. This is because it is very similar to the step and differentiable function in the vicinity of any point of the x-axis. As will be seen, this is necessary in the backpropagation algorithm as it is based on minimizing the error with respect to the value of the weights, so that must be derived and equal to zero.

The learning algorithm for an isolated Perceptron is as follows:

where,

1. W = weight vector.
2. k = current iteration.
3. h = learning factor.
4. X = input vector.
5. d = desired output.
6. y = output obtained in iteration k.

A very important property of this algorithm is the convergence in the presence of solution and the possibility of implementing limit cycles in the absence thereof.

H factor learning algorithm determines the speed but also accuracy. The higher, we will need fewer iterations (before we reach the vicinity of the minimum error evaluation) but learning is very rude (more likely for us to be hovering near the minimum evaluation error that actually reach). The smaller, slower but more it is fine in learning. Therefore it is necessary to reach a compromise.

1.5.2. Backpropagation

Then it will be explained the method used to train a multilayer perceptron.

1.5.2.1. Algorithm

Learning a Multilayer Perceptron is more complex. As noted above, this type of training Neural Networks is a supervised training. a set of pairs of patterns (Xi, Yi) training is defined and an error function (difference between the desired output and the obtained) is defined. Once the error obtained weights are updated to minimize it. The procedure used is the decrease in the gradient direction: a highly efficient way to implement it by an equivalent procedure to compute the Net back. This results in the back-propagation algorithm:

$$E_T = \sum_{p=1}^{P} E_p = \frac{1}{2} \sum_{p=1}^{P} \left(d_p - O_p^S\right)^2$$

where,

1. ET = total output error.

2. Ep = p output error.
3. P = number of neurons in the last layer.
4. OpS = output obtained in the neuron p S-layer (the output).
5. dp = expected output neuron p.

The learning algorithm is:

$$\omega_{ij}^{L}(k+1) = \omega_{ij}^{L}(k) - \mu \frac{\partial E_T}{\partial \omega_{ij}^{L}(k)}$$

where,

1. wijL = weight of i input neuron j in the layer L.
2. k = current iteration.
3. m = learning factor.

The resulting error is equivalent to:

$$\frac{\partial E_T}{\partial \omega_{ij}^{L}(k)} = \sum_{p=1}^{P} \frac{\partial E_p}{\partial \omega_{ij}^{L}(k)}$$

The output is a sigmoid function of the linear combination of the input variables:

$$O_j^L = \frac{1}{1+e^{-y_j^L}}; \; y_j^L = \sum_{i=1}^{N_L} \omega_{ij}^L O_i^{L-1}$$

where,

1. NL = number of neurons in the layer L.
2. Ojl = output neuron j of the layer L.
3. YJL = activation state of the neuron j of layer L.

$$\frac{\partial E_T}{\partial \omega_{ij}^{L}(k)} = \frac{\partial E_T}{\partial O_j^L} \frac{\partial O_j^L}{\partial y_j^L} \frac{\partial y_j^L \partial}{\partial \omega_{ij}^{L}(k)}$$

$$\frac{\partial O_j^L}{\partial y_j^L} = \frac{e^{-y_j^L}}{(1+e^{-y_j^L})^2} = \frac{1}{1+e^{-y_j^L}} \frac{e^{-y_j^L}}{1+e^{-y_j^L}} = O_j^L(1-O_j^L)$$

where, ii = input i Network.

For the last layer:

$$\left.\frac{\partial E_T}{\partial O_j^L}\right|_{L=S} = -(d_j - O_j^S) \rightarrow \frac{\partial E_T}{\partial y_j^S} = -(d_j - O_j^S)O_j^S(1-O_j^S) =$$

$$-(d_j - O_j^S)f'(y_j^S)\delta_j^S$$

where, δ_j^S = error signal.

For the other layers, when the output varies from one neuron affects the output neurons of the next layer:

$$\frac{\partial E_T}{\partial O_j^L} = \frac{\partial E_T}{\partial y_1^{L+1}}\frac{\partial y_1^{L+1}}{\partial O_j^L} + \frac{\partial E_T}{\partial y_2^{L+1}}\frac{\partial y_2^{L+1}}{\partial O_j^L} + \cdots + \frac{\partial E_T}{\partial y_{N_L+1}^{L+1}}\frac{\partial y_{N_L+1}^{L+1}}{\partial O_j^L} =$$

$$\sum_{i=1}^{N_L+1} \frac{\partial E_T}{\partial y_i^{L+1}}\frac{\partial y_i^{L+1}}{\partial O_j^L} = \sum_{i=1}^{N_L+1} \delta_i^{L+1} \partial \omega_{ij}^{L+1}(k)$$

$$\rightarrow \frac{\partial E_T}{\partial y_j^L} = O_j^L(1 - O_j^L) \sum_{i=1}^{N_L+1} \delta_i^{L+1} \partial \omega_{ij}^{L+1}(k) = f'(y_j^L) \sum_{i=1}^{N_L+1} \delta_i^{L+1} \partial \omega_{ij}^{L+1}(k)$$

In short, the weights update algorithm is:

$$\omega_{ij}^L(k+1) = \omega_{ij}^L(k) - \mu\left(O_i^{L-1}\right)\delta_j^L$$

where, the error signals are:

$$\delta_j^L = -f'(y_j^S)(d_j - O_j^S)$$

$$\delta_j^L = f'(y_j^L) \sum_{i=1}^{N_L+1} \delta_i^{L+1} \partial \omega_{ij}^{L+1}(k)$$

1.5.2.1.1. Steps of the Algorithm

The steps to follow are:

- Initialize weights and thresholds.
- Present new and desired output pattern.
- Calculate output of all network nodes.
- Calculating error signals all nodes: nodes output nodes first layer.
- Adjust weights based on error signals.
- Go to step 2.

1.5.2.1.2. Improvements and Variants

You can make some improvements to this algorithm intended to ensure convergence or make the process faster:

- *Initialization weights:* focused on convergence.
- *Learning factor:* focused on convergence.
- *Network size:* focused on generalization.

- *Term time:* focused on obtaining local minima in the error function and accelerate the process.

$$\omega_{ij}^{L}(k+1) = \omega_{ij}^{L}(k) - \mu\left(O_i^{L-1}\right)\delta_j^{L}$$

1.5.3. Features of Multilayer Perceptron

Finally, include some of the features of this type of Neural Networks from [12]:

1. It can approximate any continuous function Y = F (X) with compact support to a given accuracy.
2. Generalizes the response to new input patterns (based on approximation/interpolation).
3. Ideal when we know what we want to achieve but not how to do it and we also have reference standards: we want to generalize to new patterns.
4. Applications:
   - Pattern Recognition:
     - Character recognition in images.
     - Voice recognition phonemes.
   - Time series prediction (claims, etc.):
     - Identification and control systems.
     - Image compression and reduced dimensionality, etc.

In the case of continuous Hopfield networks (Figure 2.16) is real values in the range [-1, + 1] or [0.1]. In both cases, the activation function of neurons is sigmoidal. If working with values between –1 and +1, the function used is the hyperbolic tangent:

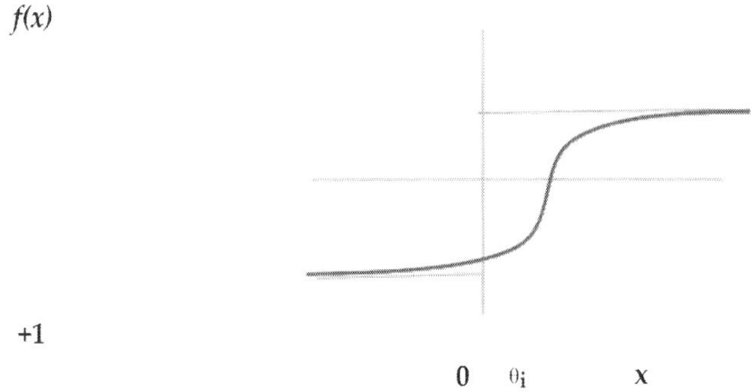

Figure 2.16. Function Activation of a Network Continuing [-1, + 1], (*Source: self-made or CC-BY license*).

If the range is [0,1] (Figure 2.17), the same function is used for the backpropagation network that:

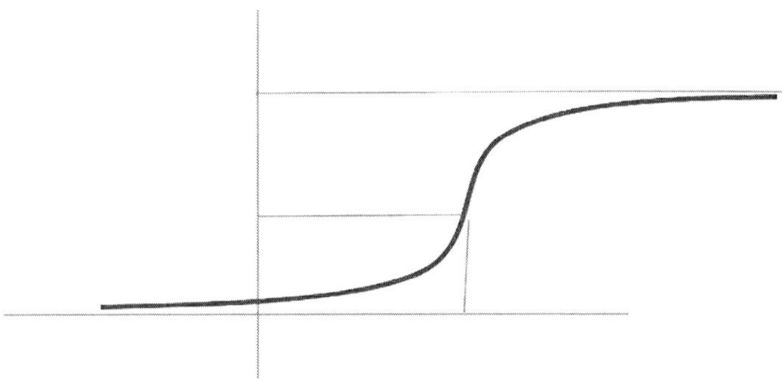

Figure 2.17. Function activation of a network, continuous [0, + 1], (Source: self-made or CC-BY license).

In either case, α is a parameter that determines the slope of the sigmoid function.

2.4.2.2. Functioning

One feature Hopfield model is that is an auto-associative network. Thus, several different patterns can be stored on a network as if it were a memory, during the learning stage. Subsequently, if presented to an entry of stored patterns, the network evolves to stabilize, then offering on the output stored information, which coincides with the one presented at the entrance. If, on the other hand, the input information does not match any of the stored, being distorted or incomplete, the network evolves as the closest exit

The information received this network must have been previously coded and represented in vector form (such as a binary configuration if the network is discrete, and as a set of real values if it is continuous) with as many components as neurons (N) having network.

This information is applied directly to the single layer consisting network, being received by the neurons of said layer (each neuron receives a part of the information, an element of the vector representing this information). If we consider in principle the case of a particular neuron network, this neuron receive as input the outputs of each of the other neurons, initially values that match the input, multiplied by the weights of the corresponding connections. The sum of these values constitute the value net input of the neuron, which will be applied the transfer function, yielding the corresponding output value, or 0/1, –1/+1 if the network is discrete, and real number in the range [0,1] or [–1, + 1] if it is continuous.

The above description corresponds to a first step in the processing performed by the network. This process continues until the outputs of the neurons are stabilized, which will happen when you stop changing value. Then, all of these (N) output values of all neurons constituting the output information generated by the network, that correspond to any of the patterns during the learning phase were stored therein.

This operation can be expressed mathematically as follows:

- 1st: At the initial instant (t = 0) input information (values applied e_1, e_2, ..., e_N).

  Initially, the output neuron matches the information applied to the input.
- 2nd: The network iterates until convergence to $s_1(T + 1)$ is equal as $_i(T)$.

where f is the transfer function (activation) of the neurons in the network. In the case of discrete model, if working with binary values output would be obtained according to the step function.

The process is repeated until the outputs of neurons remain for some iterations changes. At that moment, the output ($s_i(T + 1)$) represents the information stored by the network over the information presented on the input appears ($e_1, e_2, ..., e_N$).

Described operation corresponds to a classical discrete Hopfield network as it works with information or binary patterns. However, there is a variation model also developed by Hopfield which aims to look a little further operation of real neurons, it is continuous Hopfield network, activation functions of neurons sigmoidal, which offers more possibilities than the above, and to store patterns formed by actual values (e.g., images in color or black and white with different shades of gray) and facilitates the resolution of certain general optimization problems.

Both in this case as in the discrete network you can distinguish different versions of the model based on the temporal form in which takes place generalization or updating outputs of neurons in the network. If this update is performed simultaneously in all neurons, it is a Hopfield network with parallel operation or synchronous, since it is assumed that all neurons are able to operate synchronized and therefore the output is generated to while for all of them in each iteration, so that the next iteration (t + 1) all to be used as inputs the outputs generated by the other in the previous time (t). If, on the other hand, neurons work sequentially or asynchronously. In this case,

It is also possible, only used in continuous Hopfield networks, working with non-binary values that the generation of the output of all neurons is performed simultaneously (synchronous) and continuous in time. In this case, the operation of the network should be represented as a differential equation where f is the activation function of the neurons that will sigmoidal curves yt_i is a parameter called rate delay, which is intended to represent a biological characteristic of neurons, as is the delay that occurs in reception by a neuron i of output values generated by other neurons to which it is connected.

The Hopfield network has a mechanism offline learning. Therefore, there is a layer of learning and other network performance. In the learning stage, the values of the weights are set based on the information that is intended to memorize or store network. Once established, the network comes into operation.

This network uses a learning unsupervised Hebbian type, so that the weight of a connection between a neuron i and other j is obtained by the product of the components i-th and j-th vector information or pattern represents to be stored. If the number of patterns to be learned is M, the final value of each of the weights is obtained by the sum of the M products obtained by the above process, a product for storing information.

In the case of discrete Hopfield network, working with values –1/+ 1, this learning algorithm can be expressed as follows.

Being:

w_{ij}: Weight associated with the connection between the neuron j neuron i, which coincides with w_{ji}.

and$_{i\,(k)}$: Value of the i-th component of the vector corresponding to the k-th information should learn the network.

N: Number of neurons in the network, and therefore the size of training vectors.

M: Number of information or patterns that must learn the network.

If Network 0/1 labor with discrete values instead of –1/1, then the weights are calculated according to the expression:

In order to reach the global understanding of Artificial Neural Networks, we adopt the next perspective, called top-down starting with the *application.* It is passed to the algorithm and architecture here (Figure 2.18).

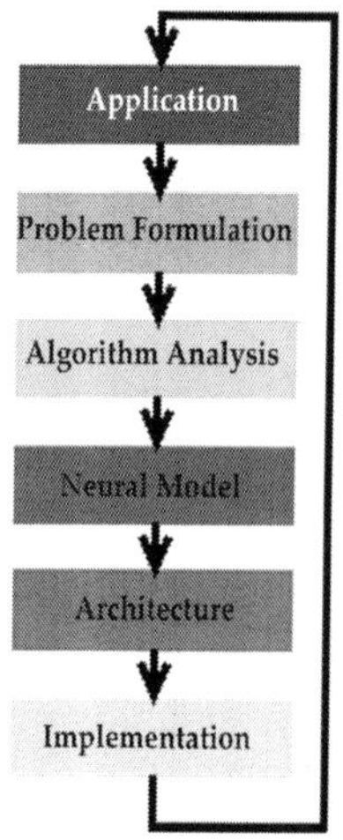

Figure 2.18. The approach to artificial Neural Networks, (*Source: self-made or CC-BY license*).

This approach to artificial Neural Networks is motivated by the application, based on the theory and implementation-oriented. The main applications are for signal processing and pattern recognition.

The first stage algorithmic represents a combination of the mathematical theory and heuristic reasoning for neural models. The ultimate goal is to build digital neuro, with the help of VLSI technologies and adaptive, digital and parallel processing.

From the point of view of applications, the advantage of the RRNN lies in parallel, adaptive and nonlinear processing. The RRNN have found many successful applications in artificial vision, signal processing and images, speech recognition and character, expert systems, medical image analysis, remote control, robot control, industrial inspection and scientific exploration. The domain of application of the RRNN can be classified as follows: association and classification, Regeneration patterns, regression and generalization, Y optimization.

2.5. ASSOCIATION AND CLASSIFICATION

In this application, input static patterns or temporal signals should be classified or recognized. Ideally, a classifier should be trained so that when given a slightly distorted version of the pattern to be recognized properly without problems. Likewise, the network should provide some immunity against noise, that is, should be able to recover a "clean" signal environments or noisy channels. This is critical in the holographic, associative or regenerative applications.

Association: Of particular interest are the two kinds of association: self-association and hetero-association. The problem of self-association is entirely recover a pattern given partial information of the desired pattern. The hetero-association is to recover a set of patterns B, given a pattern that set. Weights in associative networks are often predetermined based on the rule Hebb. Normally, the autocorrelation set stored patterns determines the weights in the auto-associative networks. On the other hand, the cross-correlation of many pairs of patterns used to determine the weights hetero-association network.

Unsupervised classification: For this application, the synaptic weights of the network are trained by the unsupervised learning rule. That is, the network adjusts the weights and verify the result based solely on the input patterns.

Supervised classification: This classification adopts some forms of interpolation or approximation criterion. Classification in many applications, such as voice recognition, training data consist of pairs of input and output patterns. In this case, it is desirable monitored networks, as well known and studied backpropagation networks. Such networks are suitable for applications that have a lot of classes with complex separation limits.

2.5.1. Complete Patterns

In many classification problems, an issue to resolve is the recovery information, i.e., recover the original pattern given only partial information. There are two kinds of problems: temporal and static. Proper use of textual information is the key to success in recognition.

2.5.2. Generalization

Generalization. It can be extended to an interpolation problem. The system is trained by a large set of samples based on a supervised learning procedure training. A network is considered to be trained successfully if you can approximate the values of the training patterns and can give "soft" interpolations for the untrained data space. The aim of Generalization is to correct the output for input stimulus that has not been trained earlier response. The system should induce salient feature of the stimulus to the input and detect regularity. Such ability to discover this regularity is critical in many applications. This makes the system work efficiently throughout the space. It has even been trained by a limited set of examples. We can see in the Figure 2.19.

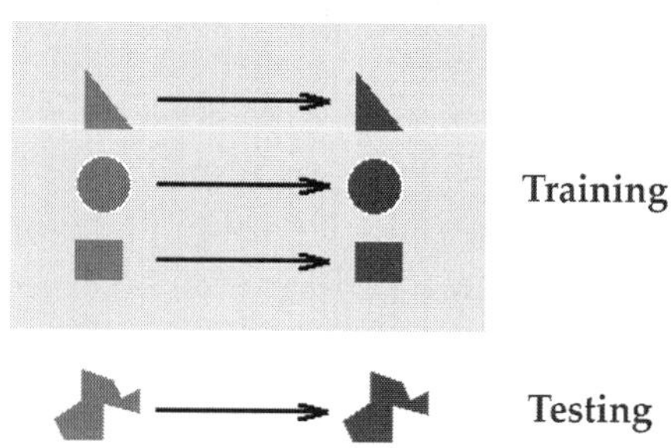

Figure 2.19. Training and testing phase, (*Source: self-made or CC-BY license*).

2.5.3. Optimization

The RRNN are an interesting tool for optimizing applications that normally involve finding the absolute minimum of an energy function (Figure 2.20).

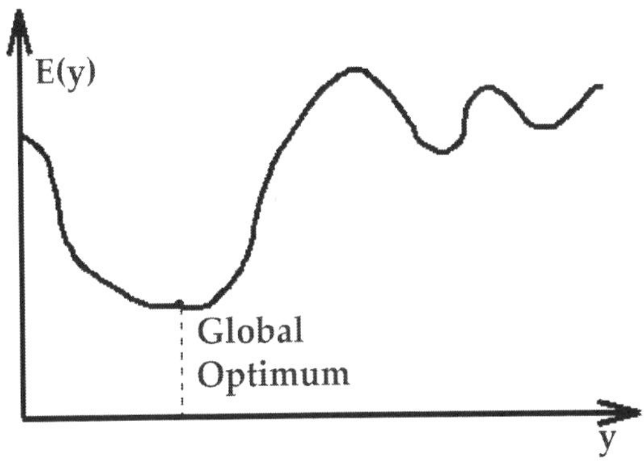

Figure 2.20. The finding of the global optimum, (*Source: self-made or CC-BY license*).

Once the energy function is defined, then the determination of the synaptic weights is done quickly. For some applications, the energy function is easily deductible. In others, however, this energy function is obtained from certain criteria of cost and special limitations. The biggest problem associated with the optimization problem is the high possibility of converging towards a local minimum rather than to the absolute minimum. To combat this problem some proposals statistics are used, such as stochastic processes.

2.5.4. Examples of Applications Artificial Neural Networks

Before noting some of the examples where Neural Networks have an important application, we can say that we focus on those who may have more relevance in our field, Computer Engineering:

2.6. NATURAL LANGUAGE PROCESSING

Natural language processing represents the process of converting written text spoken language.

NETtalk (artificial neural network) takes as inputs and as outputs texts desired codes chosen to represent the corresponding phonemes. By using a synthesizer (DECtalk) codes are transformed into phonemes. During the learning process, it was observed as was improving its ability baby from a level to the level of a 6-year-old learning to make difficult distinctions as uttering a mild or strong c depending on the context. While this had been achieved before, the most important novelty is that by the Neural Network is not necessary to define and schedule a lot of complex rules, because the network automatically extracts the necessary knowledge.

2.6.1. Learning Grammars

Rumelhart and McClelland [25] studied how we build the rules about language, and tried to teach a Neural Network last of the English verbs. The system was improved and eventually was able to generalize and conjugating verbs unknown.

2.6.2. Image Compression

Cottrell et al. [26], have achieved encode images with a compression ratio of up to 8: 1 without devising any rules and high fidelity reconstruction.

2.6.3. Character Recognition

2.6.3.1. Handwriting Recognition

Nestor, Inc => read what is written by a graphics card. After learning, they are able to recognize deeds they had never seen before. It has been used for example to recognize kanji (Japanese writing), eliminating the great difficulty of this language to introduce it into the computer.

The neocognitron (Kunihiko Fukishima) simulates how the visual information is moving in the cerebral cortex. Get an advanced pattern recognition with great capacity for abstraction and generalization that make it able to recognize patterns with different orientation and high levels of distortion.

2.6.4. Pattern Recognition in Images

2.6.4.1. Classification of Objectives

In this field have developed numerous applications such as image classification sonar and radar, detection of cancer cells, neurological and cardiac lesions, geological surveys, etc. They are very useful to process images that do not know well what the essential or distinctive characteristics because the networks do not need to have prior explicit rules for classification, but draw the necessary knowledge.

2.6.4.2. Machine Vision Industrial Robots

For example, for label inspection, sorting of components, etc. Outperforms other vision systems also minimizes the requirements of operators and facilitates maintenance.

2.6.4.3. Noise Filter

Artificial Neural Networks are better preserving the deep structure and detail than traditional filters when eliminate noise. The first professional application of Neural Networks consisted of a filter to remove noise on the phone lines.

2.6.4.4. Combinatorial Problems

Artificial Neural Networks are offering some hope in the area algorithmically complex problems such as NP-complete; for example, the problem of the traveling salesman (Hopfield & Tank [27]).

2.6.4.5. Other Applications

2.6.4.5.1. Modeling and Prediction of Economic Indicators

Best results are obtained with any other known method (such as programs moving average). It has been applied for example to the prediction of interest rates, trade deficits, stock prices, etc.

2.6.4.6. Tory

In 1956 the first conference was held in Dartmouth IA. Here the potential use of computers to simulate discussed "every aspect of learning or any other feature of intelligence" and the first simulation of a Neural Network was presented, although not yet know to interpret the resulting data.

In 1959, **Widrow** published a theory of neural adaptation and patterns inspired by this theory, Adaline (Adaptive Linear Neuron) and Madaline (Multiple Adaline). These models were used in numerous applications and allowed use for the first time, a Neural Network in an important real-world problem: adaptive filters to eliminate echoes in telephone lines.

1962, **Rosenblatt** publishes the results of an ambitious research project, the development of Perceptron, an identifier of binary optical patterns and binary output. Perceptron capabilities extended to develop the delta rule learning, allowing employ continuous signals input and output.

In 1969, **Minsky** & **Papert** made a serious criticism of Perceptron, revealing serious limitations such as inability to represent XOR, because of its linear nature. This work created serious doubts about the capabilities of connectionist models and led to a plummeting of investigations.

Despite the blow that marked the work of Minsky and Papert for research in connectionist computing, a handful of researchers continued to work and develop new ideas: **Anderson** studies and develops models of associative memories. Stresses autoasociador linear model known as brain-state-in-a-box (BSB).

Kohonen & Anderson continues to work and develop competitive learning models based on the principle of lateral inhibition. Its main contribution is a method for physically adjacent units learn to represent similar input patterns; networks based on this method are called Kohonen networks.

Grossberg did important theoretical work – mathematical trying based on physiological principles; He contributed important innovations with its model ART (Adaptive Resonance Theory) and, along with Cohen, made an important theorem on the stability of recurrent networks in terms of an energy function.

In the 80s, in this decade the revival of interest in the field is produced thanks mainly to the work of the group PDP Hopfield and contributions.

Rumelhart, McClelland & Hinton created a group called PDP (Parallel Distributed Processing). As a result of the work of this group came the most influential manuals from Minsky and Papert criticism. He stresses the chapter backpropagation algorithm, which solves the problems raised by Minsky and Papert and greatly extends the scope of connectionist computing models.

Hopfield develops a model consisting of interconnected units that reach minimum energy process, using the principles developed by Grossberg stability network. The Hopfield model was very illustrative of the mechanisms of storage and retrieval of memory. His enthusiasm and clarity of presentation gave a new impetus to the country and led to increased research.

Other notable developments of this decade are the Boltzmann machine and models BAM.

2.7. NETWORK LAYER: PERCEPTRON, ADALINE, AND MADALINE

2.7.1. Perceptron Background

In 1943, Warren and Walter Pitts McCulloch originated the first model of neuronal operation, which was improved in its biological Donald Hebb in 1948.

In 1962, Bernard Widrow proposed learning rule Widrow-Hoff and Frank Rosenblatt developed a convergence test, and defined the range of problems for which its algorithm ensured a solution. He proposed the 'Perceptrons' as a computational tool.

2.7.2. Functioning

The following figure shows an "artificial" neuron, which attempts to model the behavior of the biological neuron is represented. Here the body of the neuron is represented as a linear adder of zj external stimuli, followed by a nonlinear j = f (zj) function. The function f (zj) is called the activation function, and the function using the sum of stimuli to determine the activity of the neuron output.

We see in detail in the following illustration (Figure 2.21):

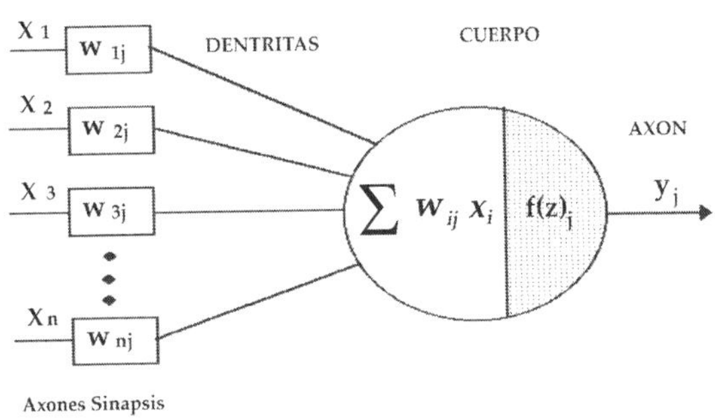

Figure 2.21. Perceptron model, (*Source: self-made or CC-BY license*).

This model is called McCulloch-Pitts perceptron, and is the basis of most of the architecture of RNA that are interconnected with each other. Neurons use different activation functions depending on the application, sometimes are linear functions, other sigmoidal functions (e.g., tanh – hyperbolic tangent), and other functions threshold. Synaptic efficacy is represented by weighting factors wij interconnection from neuron i, to neuron j.

The weights may be positive (excitation) or negative (inhibition). Weights along with the functions f (z) dictate the operation of the Neural Network. Usually, functions are not changed so that the state of the Neural Network depends on the value of the weight factors (synapses) applied to stimuli Neuron.

In a perceptron, each entry is multiplied by the corresponding weight W, and the results are summed and are evaluated against the threshold value, if the result is higher than the same, the perceptron is activated.

2.7.3. Restraining

The perceptron is able to solve only a hyperplane defined functions (N-dimension object 1 contained in a space of dimension N). That cutting dimensional space N. An example of a function that cannot be resolved is the XOR logical operator.

A simpler explanation would be a hyperplane, speaking in a two dimensional plane, a line that separates the existing elements into two groups. The perceptron can only solve a function, if all possible outcomes of the problem can be separated in this way (in two sections) i.e., not combined with each other.

2.7.4. Training

Training a Perceptron is through the delta learning rule:

For each weight W dW one adjustment is made according to the rule:

dW = LR (T – Y) X

Where LR is the reason for learning, T the desired value, and the value obtained, and X input applied to the perceptron.

2.7.5. Types of Perceptron

The basic Perceptron two layers (input linear neurons, analog, and output with activation function step-type digital) could only establish two separate linear boundary in the pattern space entry regions where have a hyperplane.

A Perceptron with three levels of neurons can form any convex region in this space. Convex regions are formed by regions formed insight among each neuron of the second layer, each of these elements behaves like a simple perceptron, activating its output patterns one side of the hyperplane.

A four-layer Perceptron can generate arbitrarily complex decision regions. The separation process in classes is carried out involves the partition of the desired region in small hypercubes.

Each hypercube requires 2n neurons in the second layer (the number of inputs n being the network), one on each side of the hypercube, and one in the third layer, which performs the logical AND of the output node level previous. Output nodes of this third level will be activated only for the inputs of each hypercube. Hypercubes are assigned to the region right decision by connecting the output of each node of the third level only with the output neuron (fourth layer) corresponding to the region decision that this comprised the hypercube carrying out an operation OR logic in each output node. This procedure could be generalized so that the shape of the convex regions is arbitrary, rather than hypercubes. In theory, Perceptron 4 layer can solve a variety of problems whose inputs are analog, the output is digital and is linearly separable. The practical problem is the number of neurons in the appropriate number of hidden layers, the extent of the activation function, training time network, the implications noise generation (having an excessive number of neurons) in contrast with the advantage of having a fault tolerant system having a number of redundant neurons.

2.7.6. Perceptron Applications

The range of tasks that can handle Perceptron is much greater than simple decisions and pattern recognition. For example, you can train a network to form the past tense of verbs in English, read English and handwritten text. The Multilayer Perceptron (MLP) may be used to predict a series of data over time. It has been such a success in measuring demand for gas and electricity, as well as predicting changes in the value of financial instruments.

Predicting financial markets, medical diagnoses, as a coding Perceptron network, Perceptron learns to add integers.

Nettalk, implementation of which we have discussed above, is a Perceptron which is capable of transforming text into English in individual sound (phonetic representations) and pronunciation with the use of a speech synthesizer; It has approximately 300 neurons nodes (being 80 in the hidden layer) and 20,000 individual connections.

2.7.7. Perceptron Algorithm

The goal is to find a perceptron for calculating a function of n-variables that have a file of examples, i.e., a series of lines, where each line represents an example:

x_1, x_n, and *x_2 ...*

with the values of the entries, X_i followed by the value and function to those entries.

To find the perceptron have to "learn" w_i weights associated with each input variable

X_i + b = the bias W_n + 1 (that would be the -threshold).

So that the function will calculate the Perceptron:

Y = f (e)

It is and the stimulus that enters the perceptron function f activation thereof:

*e = b + Σ x_i * w_i* and

f (x) = 1/(1 + e x)

In the event that the output was binary function would:

Y = 1 iff (e)> 0.5, and

Y = 0 if f (e) <0.5.

And in case that it take n discrete values would generalize this by dividing the unit interval [0,1] into n subintervals (1 for each value).

It is assumed that the file is normalized and thus, both Y and each X_i takes values between 0 and 1. Otherwise had previously normalize said interval.

What is intended is to minimize the mean square error

(Σ Error ^ 2)/No examples)

by the technique of decreasing gradient

2.7.7.1. Constant

l (Learning rate, usually between 0.01 and 0.1)

E (root mean square error admitted)

Nº Max Iteraciones (Maximum iterations we will give)

2.7.7.2. Variables

I (number of iterations)

K (counter examples)

W [i: 1..n + 1] (weights perceptron)

X [i: 1..n] (input values in the present example)

Y (output value in the current example)

SP (perceptron output to the input of current example)

Error (error in the current example)

ECM (mean square error)

Step 1: Initialize Variables

I = 0;
I = 1..n to + 1

W [i] = <*no random* (Typically between –1 and 1)> (very important that the random number is,

different in each run)

ECM = E

Step 2: Loop Iterations

While (I <N°MaxIteraciones) and (ErrorCuadraticoMedio> E)

Step 2.1: Loop passing through all Examples

Open (<file examples>)

K = 0

While not in the end of file

Read Values Example

Read (x [i] (i = 1..n), and)

Calculate error in this example

SP = W [n + 1] + Σ x [i] * W [i] (output input perceptron example h)

SP = 1/(1 + e ^ (- SP))

Error = y – SP (Difference between the value of h and the SP example)

Update weights according to the error of that example

Update entries weights

For each i = 1..n

W [i] = *W [i]* + γ * SP * (1-P) * x [i] * Error

Update bias (= -threshold)

W [n + 1] = *W [n + 1]* + γ * SP * (1–P) * Error

Increase counter examples

k = k + 1

Close (<file examples>)

Step 2.2: Calculate Mean Square Error

ECM = 0;

Open (<file examples>)

While not in the end of file

Read (x [i] (i = 1..n), and)

SP = *W [n + 1]* + Σ x [i] * W [i]

SP = 1/(1 + e ^ (- SP))

Error = y – SP

ECM + = ECM (Error) ^ 2

ECM = ECM/k

Close (<file examples>)

Step 2.3: Increase Iteration Counter

I = I + 1

Step 3: Output

Write ("The Perceptron is learned pesos")

For i = 1..n

Write ("W" i "=" W [i])

Write ("BIAS =" W [n + 1])

It is one of the simplest neural structures along with the Perceptron.

It consists of a single processing element (Adaline: Adaptive Linear element; "Widrow-Hoff").

If several adalines combine the configuration called Madaline is obtained.

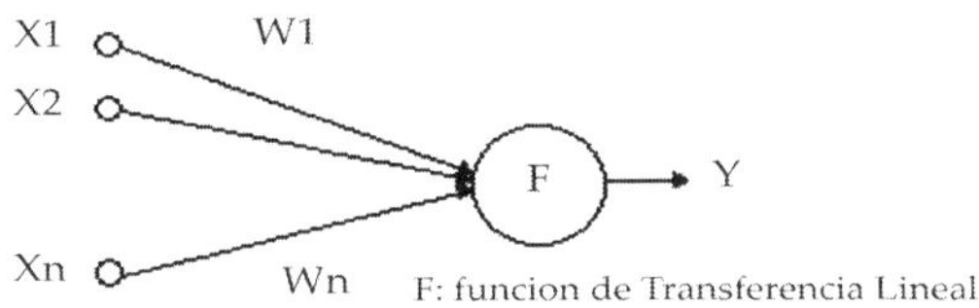

Elemento Lineal: Adaline

Training for supervised learning is used specifically for error correction. Learning is Off-Line.

$$y_j = w_{j0} + \sum_{i=1}^{n} w_{ji} * x_i$$

It is to modify the weights to try to reduce the difference between the desired output and the current (for each pattern).

The learning rule to use is called LMS: minimizes the Mean Squared Error over all the training patterns.

Optimal Weight Calculation

Be the training set (X, D) input patterns and desired outputs.

X ---- set of L vectors of dimension n.

D ---- set of L vectors of dimension m (in this case m = 1). Desired output.

Y ---- set of L vectors of dimension m (in this case m = 1). Output obtained.

This is to minimize: Sea output Yk obtained for the k pattern.

The error pattern for the k $E_k = d_k - y_k$ so :

$$< E_k^2 >= \frac{1}{L} \sum_{k=1}^{L} E_k^2 =< (d_k - y_k)^2 >$$

$$y_k = \sum_{j=0}^{n} w_j * x_j$$

The Mean Square Error:

$$< E_k^2 >= \frac{1}{L} \sum_{k=1}^{L} E_k^2 =< (d_k - y_k)^2 >$$

$$=< (d_k - w^t x_k)^2 >=< d_k^2 > +w^t < x_k x_k^t > w - 2 < d_k x_k^t > w$$

$$R = < x_k x_k^t > \quad P = < d_k x_k > \quad \xi = < E_k^2 >$$

$$\xi = < d_k^2 > + w^t R w - 2P^t w$$

To find the minimum derive with respect to W and is equal to 0:

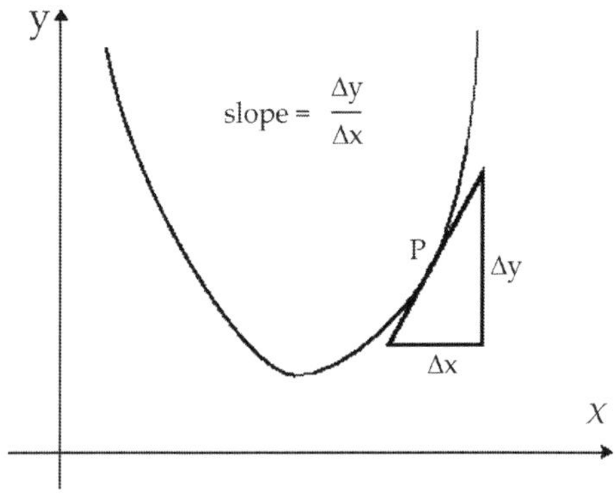

$$\frac{\nabla \xi(w)}{\nabla w} = 2Rw - 2P$$

$$2Rw^* - 2P = 0$$

$$w^* = R^{-1} P$$

Consequences:

It has one end

The end is minimal.

2.8. BACKPROPAGATION

2.8.1. Backpropagation Networks (Back-Prop)

Speaking of networks or networks backpropagation we refer to a learning algorithm rather than a specific architecture.

Backpropagation error is propagated backward, i.e., from the output layer towards the input layer, through intermediate hidden layers and adjusting connection weights in order to reduce the error.

There are different versions or rules backpropagation algorithm and different connectionist architectures that can be applied.

For a long time it was not available algorithms for training multilayer networks, and as a layer networks were very limited in what they were capable of representing the field of artificial Neural Networks was stagnant.

The invention and further the backpropagation algorithm gave a great impulse to the development of this field. It has a good mathematical foundation and despite its limitations has greatly expanded the range of problems where artificial Neural Networks are applied.

Apparently, the algorithm was devised in the early 70 Werbos, and rediscovered in the early 80 Parker and Rumelhart independently. However, it did not become popular until 1986, when Rumerlhart, Hinton, and Williams presented a clear and concise description.

And it is that at first not appreciated as he deserved. That remained forgotten for so long should also be a result of the interdisciplinary condition of the field, divided between mathematics and computer science, neuroscience and psychology.

Since the key date of 1986 has created new versions that have tried to increase the speed of convergence of the algorithm and have tried to overcome some of the drawbacks such as the tendency to local minimums and no global reach.

2.8.2. Mathematical Description of Backpropagation Algorithm

A version of the algorithm is explained (Hinton, 1992) for networks with the following characteristics:

- non-recurring.
- Activation function sigmoidal.
- fully interconnected layers.
- Fully synchronous operation.

1. We randomized the weights of the connections.
2. We are presenting an input pattern and calculate the output.
3. Given a j-th unit output layer and i-th unit of the hidden layer immediately above, calculate the total weighted input and output or activation thereof (Figure 2.22).

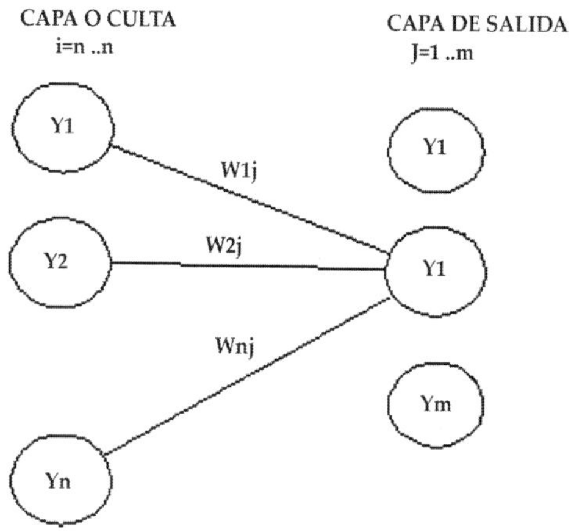

Figure 2.22. Backpropagation model, (*Source: self-made or CC-BY license*).

where,

$$x_j = \sum_{i=1}^{n} (y_i \cdot w_{ij})$$

$$y_j = \frac{1}{1+e^{-x}}$$

4. Once computed activities of all the units output an estimate of error, generally, a quadratic function of the individual errors for each unit is calculated, each individual error the difference between the desired output and obtained.

$$E = \frac{1}{2} \sum_j (d_j - y_j)^2$$

d_j being the desired output for the j-th-unit

5. Calculating the rate of change of the error changing activity of each output unit (EA, error of the activity)

$$EA_j = \frac{dE}{dy_j} = d_j - y_j$$

It is precisely the difference between the desired output and the actual output obtained, i.e., the difference between the desired activity and real activity.

6. Calculating the rate of change of the error by changing the total input it receives each output unit.

$$\delta_j = \frac{dE}{dk_j} = \frac{dE}{dy_j}\frac{dy_j}{dk_j} = EA_j y_j(1 - y_j) = y_j(1 - y_j)(d_j - y_j)$$

It is equal to the rate of change of the error by varying their activation multiplied by the rate of change of activation by changing its input (which is just the derivative of the sigmoid function).

7. Calculating the rate of change of error to be modified weighing afferent connection to an output unit.

$$EP_{ij} = \frac{dE}{dw_{ij}} = \frac{dE}{dk_j}\frac{dk_j}{dw_{ij}} = \delta_j y_i$$

It is equal to the rate of change of error to vary its input, the rate of change of the input to vary the weight.

So far we calculate the EA only for output units, what about the hidden units?. In this case, we have no direct estimate of error contributed by each hidden unit; here is where the propagation or back-propagation error (Figure 2.23):

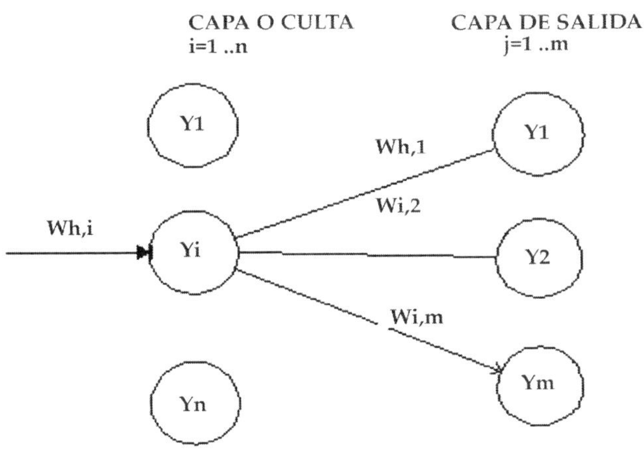

Figure 2.23. The propagation or back-propagation error, (*Source: self-made or CC-BY license*).

The i-th unit of the hidden layer affects all output units; therefore, as to estimate the error varies by varying the activity of that hidden unit, one must add the individual effects of its activity on all output neurons.

Each individual effect on the variation of the error is equal to the rate of change of the error output unit to change its total input, multiplied by the rate of change of its input to vary the activity of the hidden unit.

$$EA_i = \frac{dE}{dy_i} = \sum_{j=1}^{m} \left(\frac{dE}{dk_j} \frac{dk_j}{dy_i} \right) = \sum_{j=1}^{m} (\delta_j w_{ij})$$

8. Knowing EA for units of any layer can dy EP calculate the known expressions.

$$\delta_i = EA_i y_i (1 - y_i) = y_i (1 - y_i) \sum_{j=1}^{m} (\delta_j w_{ij})$$

$$EP_{ki} = \delta_i y_k$$

9. Arranging the rate of change of the error on the weight of a connection (EP), we can use different rules for modifying the weight in order to reduce said error.

One of the first rules that took advantage of this algorithm is the Generalized Delta Rule, Which calculates the increase applied to a weight ratio as a direct rate of change of the error and the learning coefficient h, typically with values between 0.01 and 1.0

$$\Delta w_{ij} = \mu \delta_j y_i$$

$$w_{ij}(t+1) = w_{ij}(t) + \Delta w_{ij}$$

2.8.3. Assessment

Backpropagation algorithm presents certain problems, some related to its dubious neurophysiological plausibility, and other concerning certain computational aspects, which are that we will discuss below:

- The results depend on the initial, random, values connections. This makes it convenient to train several networks with different initial values and choose the one that works best.
- Sometimes it takes a long time for simple solutions. This problem by increasing processor power and the use of new technologies is reduced, however, the computing time increases significantly with increasing network size. While the volume of calculation is proportional to the total number of connections. In practice, increasing the size of the network, we need more examples of learning, and that causes a much greater increase increases

learning time. To increase the speed of convergence have developed different modifications of the algorithm.

- "Catastrophic interference" or deterioration in system performance as a result of the addition of new learning examples.
- **Paralysis**: This happens when the weights are adjusted to very large values, that operated at the processing units with a near 1 activation, and therefore, the gradient of the error approaches 0 consequently not produce changes in the weights, learning is stopped. Therefore it is desirable to randomize the weights of the connections with small values and use the learning rate, too small, despite slowdowns in learning.
- **Temporary instability**. If we use a high coefficient of learning, they will produce large increases in the weights, so it is easy to spend increment and having to try to make up in the next cycle, so that continuous oscillations would occur. This is solved using a small coefficient, or not to have a very slow learning, said coefficient adaptively modify (increase it if the global error decreases, and decrease otherwise).
- **The problem of local minima**. The backpropagation algorithm uses a gradient descent technique, this means that follows the "error surface" always down, until a local minimum, but does not guarantee that a globally optimal solution is reached. However, it has been found that the fact does not prevent local minima achieve satisfactory results are achieved. On the other hand, methods have been developed to solve this problem, as asynchronous mode or probabilistic operation and use of statistical methods.

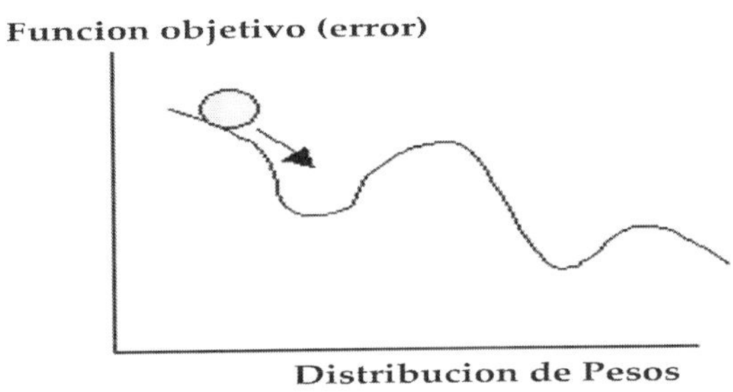

We can consider the error as an area full of slopes, if we let a ball fall into a valley, but not necessarily in the depths, but in the nearest (a local minimum).

An intuitive idea to solve this, would apply some energy to that shaking or making vibrating surface (momentum), this would jump to the ball from valley to valley, as the deepest valleys is harder to get out, you tend to be in valleys each deeper time. If we shake the surface slowly, at the end we will have the ball in the deepest valley of the surface.

Other techniques that can help avoid falling into local minima are to add some noise to changes in the weights of the connections. Another measure is to add noise to the connections, but this is more useful to give strength and increase the generalizability of the network. These measures, by contrast, increase learning time.

2.9. VALIDATION

Once we have our model, you need to try it in different situations and circumstances.

We must ensure that our network is working properly, since it could not do so for different reasons. The most common are:

- Insufficient training;
- Unrepresentative data set; and
- Overtraining.

2.9.1. Optimal Point to Stop Training

Within validation techniques, one of the main goals pursued is to find what exactly is the point at which we should stop our training.

Generally, they usually meet the following criteria:

- Arriving in evaluating a number of examples.
- When the error reaches a minimum.
- If the error reduction is conveniently provided below.

2.9.2. Simple Method Validation

This is the method known as "hold-out."

Its methodology divides the dataset into three groups, which must be clearly differentiated and conscientiously chosen:

- Data for training: are the data that will train our network, and through which learning will take place.

- Data validation: data will serve as proof that our Neural Network is working properly and in the way we expected.
- Data for test: will a small data set, chosen at random, which eventually will give a result of the work of our network.

2.9.3. Method Cross-Validation

This validation method seeks to eliminate the dependence of randomly selecting the data sets for validation.

Thus, in each series of data sets will be selected to form one part of the validation.

It produces more reliable validation, although time-consuming something higher.

2.9.4. Other Validation Methods

Simply mention other usual methods in the validation of Neural Networks:

- Bootstrapping.
- Stacked generalization.

It is very important to check that our network is working properly with some examples that has not been trained (think that, like parrots, could have learned only examples that have been trained).

To make a success of this task, we must have a set of comprehensive data adequately represent the problem that we are working with our Neural Network.

However the validation process, we have to check if our computer model is closely based on real situations that we present and to what ultimately was conceived.

3
CHAPTER

ARTIFICIAL NEURAL NETWORKS

CONTENTS

3.1. INTRODUCTION

The human mind emerges as a model for intelligent machines because in principle it is an obvious idea to imitate their behavior. A computer simulation of brain functioning has been an object of study of AI (Artificial Intelligence) since the forties of the last century. The powerful qualities of mind when it comes to thinking, memory, and problem solving, and inspired scientists trying computerized modeling operation. A group of researchers set out to create a computer model that matches the functionality of the mind in a fundamental way and the result has been the neurocomputation.

3.2. ANALOGY WITH THE BRAIN

The neuron is the fundamental unit cell of the nervous system and, in particular, the brain. Each neuron is a simple microprocessing unit that receives and combines signals from many other neurons through input process structures called dendrites. If the combined signal is strong enough, active neuron firing, producing an output signal; path signal is output on a component called an axon. This simple transfer of information has chemical nature, but has side effects that can measure electric type.

It is estimated that the brain consists of some tens of millions of densely interconnected neurons. The axon (output path of the signal) of a neuron is divided and connected to the dendrites (input route) of other neurons via a union called synapses. The transmission on this binding is chemical in nature and the amount of transferred signal depends on the amount of chemicals (called neurotransmitters) released by axon and received by the dendrites.

This synaptic efficacy (or resistance) is modified when it learns mind. The combined synapse with information processing in the neuron form the basic mechanism of memory in the brain (Figure 3.1).

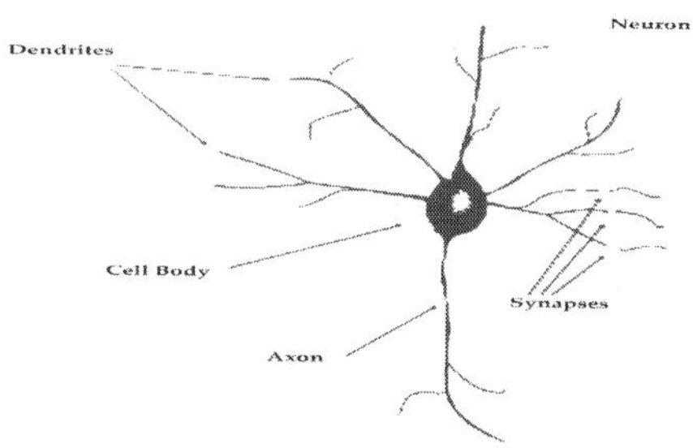

Figure 3.1. Illustrates a biological neuron, (*Source: self-made or CC-BY license*).

3.3. NEURAL NETWORKS

In an artificial Neural Network analogous to the biological neuron unit is referred to as a "node" or "processing element." A node has many inputs (dendrites) and combines, usually through a sum, the values of these entries. The result is a level of internal activity for the node. The inputs are then combined modified by a transfer function. This transfer function may be threshold type which will, pass information only if the combined level of activity reaches a certain level, or maybe a continuous function of the combination of inputs. The output value of the transfer function is generally passed directly to the output path node.

Exit path of a node may be connected to inputs of other nodes using weights corresponding (analogously) to the synaptic strength of neural connections. As each connection has a corresponding weight or weight signals input lines to a node they are modified by these weights previously before being combined. That is, the sum function is a weighted sum. In itself, this simplified model of a neuron is not very interesting; interesting effects result from the ways in which neurons are interconnected.

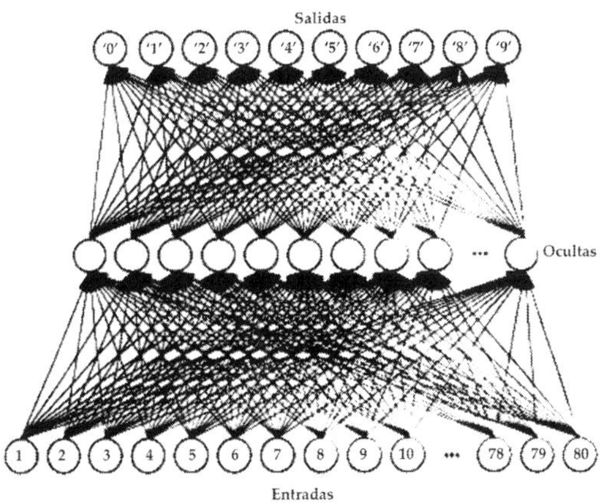

Figure 3.2. A processing element or node, (*Source: self-made or CC-BY license*).

A Neural Network consists of many nodes attached or connected to the way shown in Figure 3.2. Nodes are usually organized in groups called "layers." A typical network consists of a sequence of layers with full or random connections between successive layers.

There are usually two layers with connections to the outside world: an input buffer where data are presented to the network, and an output buffer containing the response of the network to a given input. Interlayers are called "hidden layers."

3.4. NETWORK OPERATION

There are two main phases in the operation of a network – learn and remember. In most networks this is different.

"Learning" is the process of adaptation or modification of weights in response to stimuli presented in the input layer and the output layer optionally. A stimulus presented in the output layer corresponds to a desired response due to a given input; this desired response provided by a "instructor with knowledge." In this case, learning is referred to as "supervised learning."

If the desired output is different from the input, the trained network is known as "hetero-associative network." If, for all training example, the required output vector equals the input vector, the trained network is called "auto-associative." If any required output is not displayed, learning is called "unsupervised."

A third type of learning, which falls between supervised and unsupervised, is the "reinforcement learning" where an external instructor indicates if the response is good or bad. In some instances, the network can be qualified only after some entries have been processed by the network.

Any kind of learning is used, a feature essence of every network is its "learning rule." The learning rule specifies how the weights are adapted in response to a training example. Learning may require network show many examples, many thousands of times, or only once.

The parameters that govern the learning rule may change over time as the network progresses in their learning. The long-term control parameter learning is known as a learning calendar.

"Remember" refers to how the network processes a stimulus presented in its input buffer and creates a response in its output buffer. Often remembrance is an integral part of the learning process and a desired response when the network should be compared with the actual output value to create an error signal.

The simplest form of Neural Network has no feedback connections from one layer to another or to itself. Such a network is called "feedforward network" (or something like pro-power network).

In this case, the information passes the input buffer, to intermediate layers and to the output layer, gradually, using the characteristics of the functions weighted sum and transfer of the particular network in question.

The feedforward networks are interesting because of non-linearities in the transformations. In some of these networks, a certain amount of feedback is created so that the network has time sensitivity, i.e., having temporal reference points. These networks are called recurrence or feedback.

If there are connections of feedback, information reverberate around the net on the layers or within them, until there is some convergence criterion is reached. The information is then passed to the output layer.

3.5. OPERATION OF THE LAYERS

Two operations are used in Neurocomputing can affect a network completely as a whole, these Normalization, and Competition.

Standardization: making the vector values corresponding to the output of an entire layer, and with this scale for the total output (e.g., the sum of the vector components) is a fixed value. This is done in biological connecting each element of a layer to each other element systems. These connections allow the node individually feel the total output of the layer and adjust their own conformably values. The result of the normalization is that the total activity in the layer remains approximately constant.

Competition: refers to the interaction that a node may have with each other node in the same layer. Unlike standardization, where all nodes adjust their outputs to create a set level of activity in the competition only one or a few neurons and produce an output gain. A common form of competition is when the node busiest is the only level that triggers (which means that outputs its current state).

3.6. WHAT MAKES THE DIFFERENT NEUROCOMPUTATION?

The neurocomputation differs from the common artificial intelligence and traditional computing in some important ways.

3.6.1. Learning Through Examples

Unlike traditional expert systems where the knowledge is made explicit through rules, Neural Networks generate their own rules by learning from examples shown towards them. Learning is accomplished from a training rule which adapts or modifies the connection weights of the network in response to inputs examples and (optionally) the desired outputs of those entries.

In non-supervised learning, the network is only input stimuli and the network itself is organized internally to each hidden node responds strongly to a different set of input stimuli or a set of closely related stimuli. These sets of input stimuli represent groups in the input space typically represent different real-world concepts.

In supervised learning, for each input stimulus, a stimulus desired output is presented to the network system and configures itself desired gradually toward the corresponding input/output. Such learning is usually a variant of one of three types:

- Hebbian learning: where a weight of connection of an input path into a node is increased if the input is high and if desired also output. In biological terms, this means that a neural pathway is enhanced every time it is activated synapses correlates both neurons.
- Delta Learning Rule: is based on reducing the error between the actual output of a node and the desired output by changing the weights. This is the rule that we use in our case. It should be noted that this concept is very similar to the process of least squares linear regression.
- Competitive Learning in which the processing elements compete against each other, and that you get the strongest response to a given input modifies itself to try to turn into that entry.

3.6.2. Distributed Memory Association

An important feature of Neural Networks is the way they store information. The neurocomputational memory is distributed. The connection weights are the memory units of a Neural Network. The values of the weights represent the current state of knowledge of the network. A knowledge element, represented, for example, by a pair of input/output desired, is distributed across many storage units in the network and shares these units with other memory elements stored in the knowledge network.

Neurocomputational certain associative memories are that if the trained network is presented with a partial entry, the network will choose the closest option in memory for that input, and generate an output that corresponds to an entire entry. If the network is self-associative (that is, the input is equal to the desired output for all pairs of examples used to train the network), the partial vectors introduce the input network will result in their completion.

The nature of the memory of a Neural Network leads to reasonable responses upon presentation incomplete, noisy, or unseen entries. The property is called "generalization." Quality and significance of a generalization depends on the particular application, and the type and sophistication of the network. Multilayer networks nonlinear (in particular networks "back-propagation") learn about features in their hidden layers and combine this to produce outputs. Knowledge in the hidden layers can be combined to form "smart" responses to novel stimuli.

3.6.3. Fault Tolerance

While traditional computer systems become useless by even a small amount of damage in memory, neurocomputation systems are tolerant of failures. The fault tolerance refers to the fact that most Neural Networks, if some nodes are destroyed, truncated, disabled, or altered pequeñamente connections, then the network performance degrades only slightly more.

Performance suffers, but the system is brought to abrupt failure. The neurocomputational systems are tolerant of failures because the information is not contained in one place, but is distributed throughout the system.

This feature of "graceful" degradation makes neurocomputational extremely convenient systems for applications where failure means disaster control equipment, for example, in a nuclear power plant, missile guidance, space missions, etc.

3.7. PATTERN RECOGNITION

The neurocomputational many systems are adept at pattern recognition tasks, even more than traditional experts or statistical systems.

The human ability to translate the symbols of this page into meaningful words and ideas is a form of pattern recognition.

The pattern recognition tasks require the ability to match large amounts of input data simultaneously, and then generate generalized or categorized outputs. Also, they require reasonable answers to noisy inputs.

The neurocomputational systems have these capabilities itself as the ability to learn and build unique structures for specific or particular problems, therefore, are particularly useful in pattern recognition. The ability to select combinations of features relevant to the problem, give them an advantage over those based on statistical systems. The ability to deduct these features themselves gives them an advantage over expert systems used in pattern classification. Clearly, this is the main reason why a Neural Network can be used to classify the profile of a client on a credit analysis.

3.8. POWER SYNTHESIS

Certain Neural Network can learn mapping (functional correlation) complex and continuous one or more inputs to one or more outputs. This ability to synthesize complex continuous functions is analogous to the ability of biological systems to learn coordinated movements, such as moving a leg and hit a ball.

3.9. FRANK ROSENBLATT'S PERCEPTRON

In the various texts on the subject, there are several researchers who are always referred to by their work thereon, such as McCulloch and Pitts, Minsky, Papert, Block, and the most famous Rosenblatt.

In 1957, Frank Rosenblatt at Cornell published the first major research project in neurocomputation: the development of an element called "Perceptron." Rosenblatt's perceptron caused a lot of research interest in neurocomputation.

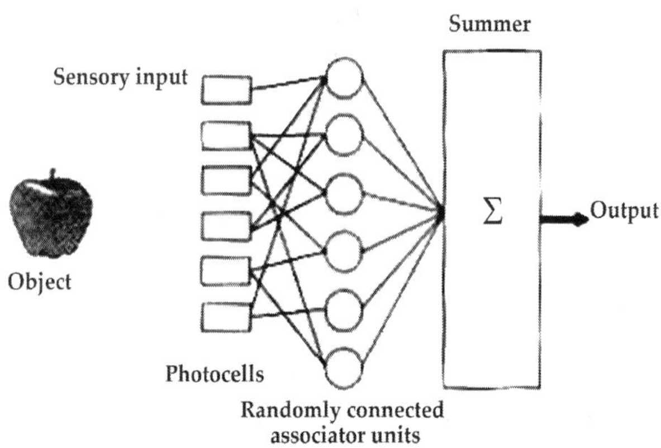

Figure 3.3. A Perceptron, (*Source: self-made or CC-BY license*).

The perceptron is a pattern classification system that can identify both abstract and geometric. The first perceptron was capable of some learning and was robust with respect to its operation was only degraded after damaging parts of its components.

The perceptron also had a large amount of plasticity, meaning that it can be restricted to a point where there is no then some cells are destroyed errors. In addition, the perceptron was able to make limited generalizations and could properly categorize patterns despite existing noise on inputs.

The perceptron was primarily targeted toward the optical pattern recognition. A grid of photocells 400, corresponding to light-sensitive retinal neurons, receiving the primary optical stimulus. These photocells were connected by polytheistic units collected electrical impulses from the photocells.

The connections between the units polytheistic collected electrical impulses were done by wiring associators randomly into cells. If the input cell exceeded a certain threshold, the association units caused a response to trigger an output.

Because developing apparatus was, the perceptron also had certain limitations. The Perceptron had no structures of states and was inappropriate for descriptions in terms of the theory of automata. Another major limitation, which would be emphasized by Minsky and Papert, was the inability of the perceptron to represent the basic problem of function Exclusive OR (XOR). Of course, this is the result of the linear nature of Perceptron.

One of the most significant changes made in the sixties after Rosenblatt has been the development of multilayer systems that can learn and categorize complex and nonlinear structures. This is typically done by using a function nonlinear transfer, but may also arise from the normalization and competition.

It is easy to see that a perceptron cannot solve linear separability. The XOR problem is illustrated in Figure 3.4. There Perceptron someone who is able to discriminate between the two groups.

This is solved by using a set of perceptrons (a network) for example, in Figure 3.4. A solution to the problem is given XOR using two perceptrons. Thus, a primitive Neural Network, as is a perceptron, can turn into a tool to discriminate patterns even if you do not have linear characteristics as XOR.

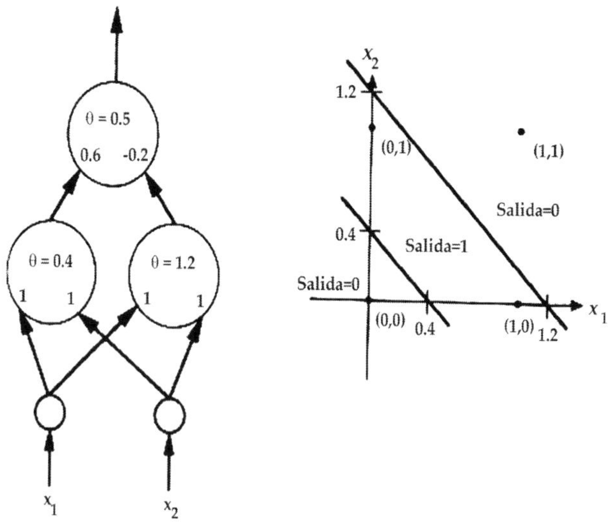

Figure 3.4. A solution to the problem XOR using two perceptrons, (*Source: self-made or CC-BY license*).

There is no straight able to separate the two groups online, but if there is able to do non-linear function. A multilayer network can emulate this behavior and that is a quality that we will use to make discrimination for credit analysis Bellsouth customers. It is also for this reason that in a previous chapter briefly described what it meant discriminant analysis.

3.10. BACKPROPAGATION

"Back-propagation "is a technique to solve the problem of credit assignment by Minsky and Papert mentioned in his book Perceptrons. David Rumelhart is a person associated with the invention of the back-propagation networks. David Parker introduced a similar algorithm almost simultaneously and others have studied similar networks.

A network of perceptrons is able to train the output nodes to learn to classify input patterns since classes are "linearly separable." More complex non-linearly separable classes can be separated with a multilayer network. However, if the output is wrong, how do we determine which node or connection set?

This is the problem of "credit assignment" (which suits us just in our particular problem). Back-propagation solves this by assuming that all processing elements and connections are guilty of some form of a wrong answer.

The responsibility for the error of the error is fixed to propagate error output back through the connections of the previous layer. This process is repeated until it reaches the input layer.

The "back-propagation" name is derived from this method of distributing the blame for the error.

3.10.1. The Backpropagation Network

The typical backpropagation network always has an input layer, a layer of outputs and at least one hidden layer. There is no theoretical limit to the number of hidden layers but typically will be one or two. Some work has been done (Figure 3.5).

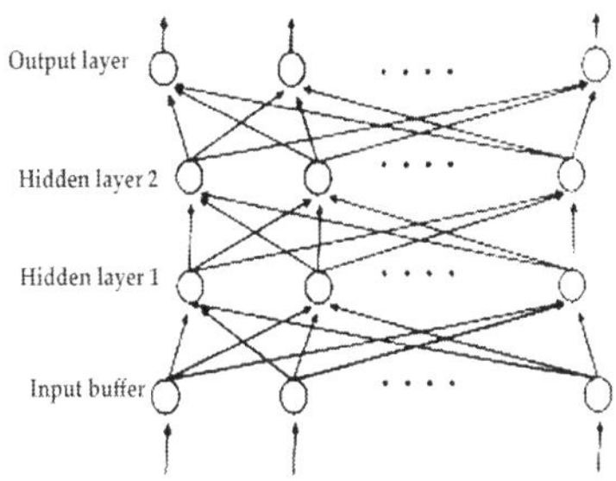

Figure 3.5. typical back-propagation network, (*Source: self-made or CC-BY license*).

indicating that up to four layers (three hidden and output) are required to solve arbitrarily complex pattern classification. Each layer is fully connected with later.

- The arrows indicate the flow of information during the recall. During learning, information is also propagated back through the network and used to update the connection weights. The network may be or hetero-associative or self-association, as mentioned above.

To avoid the confused from one layer to another, a clear notation is necessary to describe the learning rule. We use a superscript in square brackets to indicate which network layer is being considered. The rest of the notation is as follows (Figure 3.6):

1. *xj [s]* current output state of the j-th neuron in the layer s.

2. *wji [s]* weight on the connection between the i-th neuron in the layer (s-1) and the j-th neuron in the layer s.
3. *Ij [s]* weighted sum of the inputs to the j-th neuron in the layer s.

A network element backpropagation then transfers its inputs as follows:

$$x_j^{[s]} = f\left(\sum_i (w_{ji}^{[s]} \cdot x_i^{[s-1]})\right)$$

$$= f\left(I_j^{[s]}\right) \quad (1)$$

where f is traditionally the sigmoid function but can be any differentiable function. The sigmoid function is defined as

$$f(z) = \left(1.0 + e^{-z}\right)^{-1} \quad (2)$$

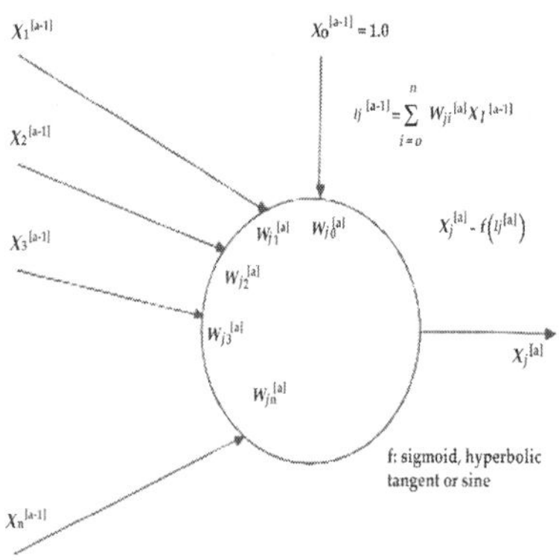

Figure 3.6. Item typical process Back-Propagation, (*Source: self-made or CC-BY license*).

3.10.2. Spreading Back the Local Error

Suppose now that the network has a global error function associated with it, which is a differentiable function of all weights in the network. Current error function is not important to understand the mechanism of reverse spread. The critical parameter is passed back through the layers is defined as

$$e_j^{[s]} = -\partial E / \partial I_j^{[s]} \quad [3]$$

We shall see later that this can be considered as a measure of local error in the j-th node at level s.

Using the chain rule twice in succession gives a relation between the local error and a particular node in the level by local errors in levels s + 1:

$$e_j^{[s]} = f'\left(I_j^{[s]}\right) \cdot \sum_k \left(e_k^{[s+1]} \cdot w_{kj}^{[s+1]}\right) \quad [4]$$

Note that the expression [4], there is a layer above the layer s; therefore, [4] it can only be used for inner layers.

If the sigmoid function defined in [2], then its derivative can be expressed as a simple function of itself as follows

$$f'(z) = f(z) \cdot (1.0 - f(z)) \quad [5]$$

Therefore, in [1], the equation [4] can be rewritten as

$$e_j^{[s]} = x_j^{[s]} \cdot \left(1.0 - x_j^{[s]}\right) \cdot \sum_k \left(e_k^{[s+1]} \cdot w_{kj}^{[s+1]}\right) \quad [6]$$

Since the transfer function is a sigmoid. The term of the sum in Ref. [6] that is used for retro-propagating errors is analogous to the summation term in Ref. [1] which is used to propagate forward through the network inputs. Then the major mechanism in a back-propagation network is spread entries for the layers to the output layer, determine the error in the output, then error propagation backward from the output layer to the input layer using [6] or more generally [4]. Multiplication error by the derivative of the transfer function scale error.

3.10.3. Minimizing Local Error

The goal of the learning process is to minimize the overall E system by modifying the weights error. This subsection will show how to do this based on knowledge of local error on each node.

Given the current set of weights wji [s], we need to determine how to increase or decrementarlas so that decreases the overall error. This can be done using a rule gradient descent a follows:

$$\nabla w_{ji}^{[s]} = -lcoef \cdot \left(\partial E / \partial w_{ji}^{[s]}\right) \quad [7]$$

where lcoef is a learning coefficient. In other words, each weight change according to the size and direction of the negative gradient in the error surface.

The partial derivatives in Ref. [7] can be calculated directly from the value of local error discussed in the previous subsection, because, by the chain rule and [1]

$$\partial E / \partial w_{ji}^{[s]} = \left(\partial E / \partial I_j^{[s]}\right) \cdot \left(\partial I_j^{[s]} / \partial w_{ji}^{[s]}\right)$$

$$= -e_j^{[s]} \cdot x_i^{[s-1]} \quad [8]$$

Combining [7] and [8], we have

$$\nabla w_{ji}^{[s]} = lcoef \cdot e_j^{[s]} \cdot x_i^{[s-1]} \quad [9]$$

3.10.4. The Global Error Function

The previous discussion assumed the existence of a global error function without specifying. This function is necessary to define the local errors in the output layer so that they can be retro-propagated into the network.

Suppose a vector is presented at the input layer of the network and suppose the desired output d is specified by an instructor. Whether or who denote the output of the network with its current set of weights. Then a measure of error achieve that desired output is given by

$$E = 0.5 \cdot \sum_k \left((d_k - o_k)^2\right) \quad [10]$$

Where the subscript k indexes the components or dy. Here, the primary local error is given by dk – ok. Expression [3], the "scaled local error" of each node in the output layer is given by

$$e_k^{(o)} = \partial E / \partial I_k^{(o)}$$

$$= \partial E / \partial o_k \cdot \partial o_k / \partial I_k$$

$$= (d_k - o_k) \cdot f'(I_k) \quad [11]$$

AND, as defined in [10], defines the global error of the network for a particular vector (i, d). A function together the global error can be defined as the sum of all the functions of specific patterns of error.

Whenever a particular vector (i, d) is shown, the back-propagation algorithm changes weights to reduce that particular component of the overall feature set of error.

3.10.5. Summary Standard Backpropagation Algorithm

Given an input vector i and a desired output d, do the following:

1. This is the input layer of the network and propagate it to the output layer to obtain an output vector o.
2. While this information is being propagated by the network, will

also prepare all entries added Ij and states xj output for each node in the network.

3. For each node in the output layer, calculate the local error scaling as in Ref. [11] and then calculating the weight using delta [9].
4. For each layer s, starting with the previous layer to the output and ending subsequent to the input, and for each node in the layer s, calculate the local error scaling as in Ref. [6] and then compute the delta weights using [9].
5. Upgrade all the weights in the network by adding the term delta to the corresponding previous pesos. This rule is called the Generalized Delta Rule which is the law of learning a backpropagation network.

3.10.6. Variations to the Standard Algorithm

3.10.6.1. Term Time

One of the problems of an algorithm gradient descent is assigned an appropriate rate of learning. The weights change as a linear function of the partial derivatives is defined as in [7] it makes the assumption that the error surface is locally linear, where "local" is defined by the size of the learning coefficient.

At points of high curvature, this assumption of linearity and no block divergent behavior can occur near the points. It is then important to keep small learning coefficient and circumvent such behavior.

Moreover small learning coefficient can lead to a slow learner. The concept of "end of time" was introduced to solve this dichotomy. The weight equation delta [9] is modified so that a portion of the previous weight delta is fed through the current weight delta:

$$\nabla w_{ji}^{[s]}(t) = lcoef \cdot e_j^{[s]} \cdot x_i^{[s-1]} + momentum \nabla w_{ji}^{[s]}(t-1) \qquad [12]$$

This acts as a filter enabling low (low-pass filter) in terms of delta weights since general trends reinforce oscillatory behavior while the gate is self. This then allows a small value for the coefficient of learning and faster learning.

3.10.6.2. Cumulative Update Weights

Another technique that has an effect on the speed of convergence is only updating the weights after pairs (input desired output) are presented to the network, rather than after each presentation. This is referred to as backward propagation accumulated (cumulative back-propagation) because the delta weights are accumulated until the entire set of pairs is presented.

The number of pairs of input/output presented during accumulation is called "time" (epoch). This may correspond either to the full set or a subset of pairs of training.

3.10.6.3. Different Transfer Functions

Instead of the sigmoid function, any "soft" function can be used as a transfer function for a processing element. Commonly this function is changed by the tangent hyperbolic, breast or linear. Recall that initially, a perceptron used a threshold function generally of (0, 1). The hyperbolic tangent is just a bipolar version of the sigmoid: the sigmoid (or logistics) is a smooth version of the threshold function (0, 1) while the hyperbolic tangent is a soft version of a threshold function (–1, 1). See Figure 3.7.

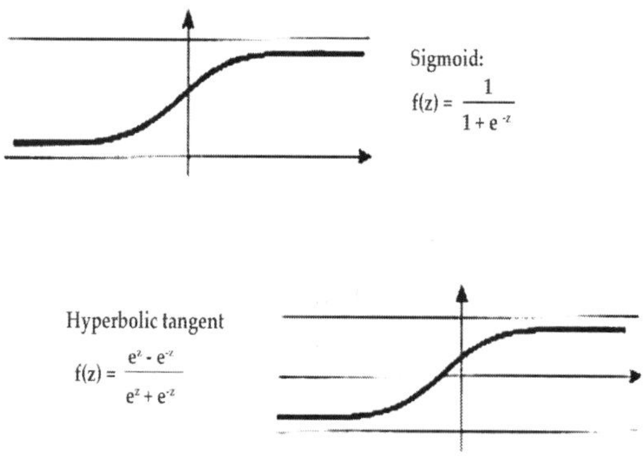

Figure 3.7. Transfer functions for backpropagation, Source: self-made or CC-BY license.

The hyperbolic tangent is defined by

$$f(z)=\frac{e^{z}-e^{-z}}{e^{z}+e^{-z}} \qquad [13]$$

As in the sigmoid function, the derivative of the hyperbolic tangent may also be expressed in terms of itself:

$$f'(z) = (1.0 + f(z)) \cdot (1.0 - f(z)) \quad [14]$$

Thus with this type of transfer function, the error function propagator [4] is changed in

$$e_j^{[s]} = \left(1.0 + x_j^{[s]}\right) \cdot \left(1.0 - x_j^{[s]}\right) \cdot \sum_k \left(e_k^{[s+1]} \cdot w_{kj}^{[s+1]}\right) \quad [15]$$

This sample as diversity results by changing the transfer functions. Much of the current neurocomputational packages suggest the transfer functions by "default." Only experience to experience and familiarity with the problem will modify the transfer functions, according to some experts.

3.10.7. Observations

All the above has only one purpose: theoretically support tool that will solve the problem of credit analysis. Much of the existing theory seeks to solve mathematical problems of nonlinear functional approaches such as the "exclusive-or" a clear case of discriminant analysis.

Networks "backpropagation" are necessarily the best option for use in determining whether a customer is or is not a good creditworthiness. This occurs primarily by the ability of the network to imitate a functional correspondence between a set input and an output.

Try to make an abstraction of the problem: a cellular operator Bellsouth attend a number of customers with different credit characteristics which can be grouped as variables in an input vector i. Also, after accepting customer credit this subject generates a record in a database collections.

Evaluating customer based on their history but we cannot say that their credit characteristics as "good payer" is the customer through his recorded in the database payments. Let these grouped into a vector d output results.

Then we would have enough to train a network of back-propagation to recognize behavior patterns of customers using their credit variables material. This is the network that, once trained, can repeat such behavior and assess a client with data sheet risk which mention is made in Chapter 1

4
CHAPTER

NEURAL NETWORKS APPLIED TO THE ANALYSIS OF IMAGES

CONTENTS

The present section shows the development of a prototype system to detect the presence of a human figure from images taken in both the controlled substance and ambient lighting.

This system has two main parts: The first is the module in which the detection object silhouette is analyzed. For this work it is necessary to differentiate the bottom of the object to be analyzed by the pixel to pixel comparison is made between two images (one containing just the background and to be analyzed); subsequently by a group is known as dilation and erosion morphological operations, noise that may be is removed; then an algorithm edge detection is applied to obtain only the outline of the object to analyze. Finally, starting from this code string travel silhouette then be used is created for the inputs to the Neural Network.

The second part is the Neural Network that is responsible for being the pattern detector, through prior training with images previously loaded into a database.

After the Neural Network has been trained and working properly, joins with the first module to create a prototype must detect the presence of a human figure based on an image group which has the operator.

The system has two types of applications: one for individual work on a computer and another based on the client/server architecture that can be used with several computers connected to a common network.

Specific Objectives

- Designing a Neural Network that has as its main qualities: easy to train, good use of resources and response times according to a security system in real time.
- Analyze the different processing techniques and select those images that facilitate the work of the Neural Network.
- Select the feature set that correctly describes the pattern you want to recognize.
- Implement the Neural Network.
- Training the Neural Network with a group of images to meet project goals.
- Integrate the elements to create a functional prototype.

Currently, we are in a society that demands more security both your home and your banks and public places, but is not willing to pay the extra money it generates. Although there are solutions to these concerns them usually are only available to a small group of people who have the money to pay them.

Usually, security systems have some surveillance cameras controlled by some operators who are often the same security guards who must perform several tasks simultaneously. Similarly, the process of watching a security camera is boring and repetitive. This causes the operator has to bear an extra load generating security flaws and may endanger what you want to monitor.

At the same time, in different sectors, they have developed more complex systems, mainly motivated by threats currently presented in a globalized world. Consequently, the field of biometrics has significantly improved to the point where it has been possible to identify different metrics that are common in humans.

One of the areas that have benefited from the development of biometrics is the identification of faces, which has not only improved the speed with which it is possible to identify a face but it is now possible to predict the natural aging of a face. Another area that is constantly improved identification of human beings either video or images to the extent that it is possible to count the number of people in the field of view of the camera and identify different measures of each of the bodies. But these developments are not available to everyone and in some cases are extremely limiting its use costs for governments and some private sectors.

For this reason, it is thought to give a simple and inexpensive solution to this problem through the creation of an autonomous system to be responsible for image analysis. This type of system has already been tested with other activities such as analysis of diagnostic imaging for disease detection, control systems for vehicle registration and compression of the handwritten letter.

In this approach, the operator is not removed but that simply provides a tool that allows you to engage in other tasks to be performed while the repetitive work is in the hands of a system that does not suffer from problems inherent in the human condition as fatigue, laziness or inattention.

To create this type of system is necessary to consider three parts, the image acquisition, image processing and classification of these. It is necessary that all these parts are properly tuned and that a failure in any of them would generate a total failure in the system.

So it is expected to create a system that meets the conditions that must be taken to detect a human figure in a group of images and to do so with low computational load without the need for a highly specialized hardware.

4.1. INTRODUCTION TO PATTERNS IN IMAGE RECOGNITION

Currently, the interest put in the hands of the process computer that previously were controlled by humans has reached a point where there are processes that cannot be easily implemented using computational techniques, as is the recognition patterns that despite so easy to us humans, is not as easy to fix as normal.

When speaking of pattern recognition, it is necessary to explain that a pattern is a set of rules that can be used to identify a particular object. Then recognize a pattern is the ability to identify objects by their similarities even though these are not fully equal to the base model.

Since for living beings pattern recognition is a relatively simple task, is not similar between different creatures, humans tend to easily recognize objects using sight as the main direction, while dogs do greater emphasis on recognition half of smell.

Using standard computer techniques is difficult to find satisfactory answers at reasonable times and it is at this point that some artificial intelligence techniques have shown one of its most important applications. Applications such as handwriting recognition, classification of objects in images, voice recognition, etc. [3].

4.1.1 Recognition of Patterns in Images

Pattern recognition in images has been of great interest to the scientific community because emulate the main sense that humans possess is of great importance to automate certain tasks that currently require vision and are highly repetitive as verification signatures, face recognition, object recognition, etc. [9].

Typically pattern recognition in images usually has the following steps: (image capture, preprocessing image, feature extraction, classification, and decision).

4.1.1.1 Capturing Images

The process by which a digital image is achieved, begins with sensors that read the intensity of light using for that different color filters and then digital memory devices that are responsible for storing the digital image, either in RGB format or as a simple information for later analysis (Figure 4.1).

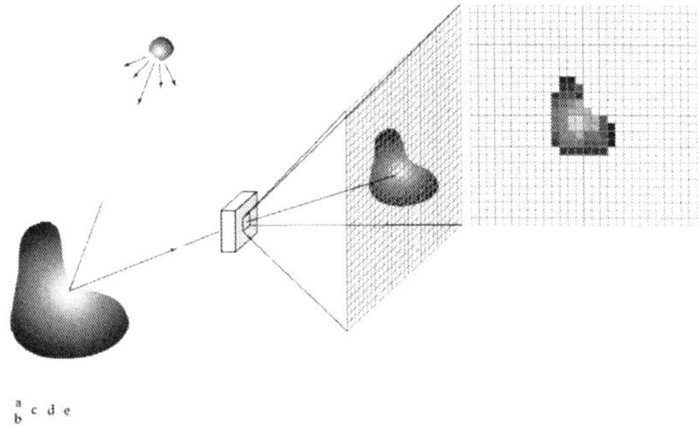

System of making images Projecting the image on a plane Element in the scene, (A) Energy (lighting), (B) element in the scene, (C) imaging system, (D) Projection of the image on a plane, (E) digital image.

Figure 4.1. An example of acquisition of a digital image, (*Source: self-made or CC-BY license*).

To create a digital image, it is necessary that a sensor captures the image, the main types of sensors are CCD (stands for charge-coupled device "device loads [electrical] interconnected") which is one of the main elements of the digital camera; This sensor is comprised of tiny photoelectric cells which record the image. Then the camera processes the image and stores it in the storage device.

There is also the APS (Active Pixel Sensor) that detects light based on CMOS technology.

4.1.1.2. Preprocessing

Although for any creature is easy to determine patterns from the image you see, computationally, it is necessary to perform image processing to be used to eliminate from it anything that might generate a fault when make a decision and this is because at the time of capturing the image the result may suffer noise, loss of quality, blur, etc.

The low-level processing, also known as pre-processing is primarily used to reduce noise, improve the contrast, etc. This type of functions can be viewed as automatic reactions that require no intelligence by the image analysis system. This process can be compared to the process of perception and adaptation suffered by a person when trying to find a seat amid the darkness of a theater, having been exposed for a period of time in the sunshine. This type of processing is characterized by the fact that both the input and output images are [4] (Figure 4.2).

Figure 4.2. Improved image contrast, (*Source: self-made or CC-BY license*).

4.1.1.3. Segmentation

The segmentation procedure partitions an image into objects or parts that constitute it. Overall, autonomous segmentation is one of the most difficult tasks in digital image processing. A process unequal segmentation generates the process to take a long time to the correct solution image problems that require objects to be individually identified.

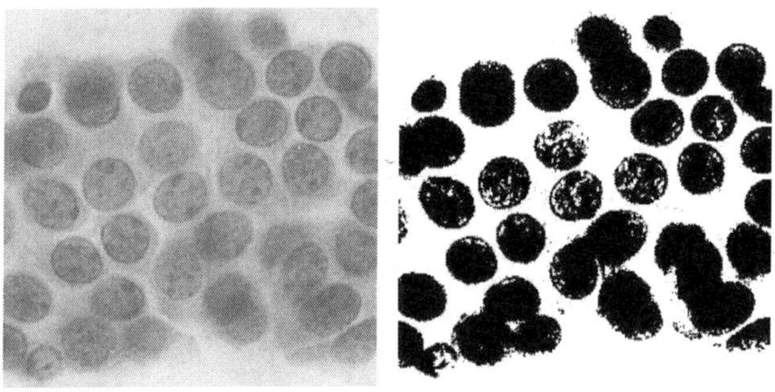

Figure 4.3. Separation of memorabilia background, (*Source: self-made or CC-BY license*).

On the other hand, a weak and erratic algorithm segmentation almost always generates an eventual failure. In general, the more successful is the segmentation, there is a greater possibility that the recognition is correct [4].

4.1.1.4. Feature Extraction

In pattern recognition feature extraction has become undoubtedly the main part as to select the features that best represent the problem, you can get the answer does not change as there are changes of light, perspective, color, etc.

Typically an image can be represented in terms of the edges of the image using either a code string or a polygonal approximation. It is also possible to represent the image based on its internal characteristics.

4.1.1.5. Classification

The ultimate goal in pattern recognition is the classification of a pattern. Using the original information with that account, it is to identify the relevant features and then remove them to measure them. These measures must pass a classifier which should be responsible for the classification, to determine which of the existing classes this pattern belongs [3].

There are different classification techniques are as follows:

- Decision Functions.
- The minimum distance classifiers.
- statistical classifiers.
- Artificial Neural Networks (ANN).
- Support vector machines (SVM).

Like any classification problem, it should be a training set which provides information necessary to associate future data entry with the decision to be taken.

4.1.1.6. Decision

From a good job in the classification process, a new entry is entered into the classifier must be in a position to give an answer that satisfies the need but the new entry is not equal to the examples used in the part of training.

It is in this part where it is checked if the above has worked correctly or if you need to change to achieve more satisfactory results. It is possible that after reaching this part, necessary to the process of classification if the answer is sought is not showing up correctly.

It is also important in this part, the results presented are easily understandable for anyone who is in charge of the system, it is possible that even though the answer is satisfactory, not understandable for a normal user. At this point, it will be necessary to discover the best way to interpret the data.

4.2. DIGITAL IMAGES

In computer terms, an image is a particular case of signal more accurately, a function that specifies a particular distribution of light intensities. In other words, an image is understood, from this point of view, as the number attributed to a two-dimensional function that assigns to all points of a segment of a plane visual values a particular value [1].

In the case of a monochromatic image, this value would be given by a simple function of two variables f (x, y), where x, y denote spatial coordinates f value at each point is proportional to the light intensity at that point or "gray level" in the case of an achromatic image. The x, y coordinates are related to a given spatial area, for example, at one end lower (x_0, Y_0) and an upper end (x_{max}, Y_{max}). In the case of a color image this value would be given by three simple functions of two variables, *fr (x, y), fg (x, y), fb (x, y),* that they express the intensity of illumination of a point x, and in the same field, and the three primary color components red (R), green (G) and blue (B). [1].

4.2.1. Basic Relationships of Pixels

Each coordinates x, y contains a pixel and it is important to note that there are some small but important relationships between each.

4.2.1.1. Neighbors of a Pixel

Each pixel p coordinate (x, y) has four horizontal and vertical neighbors you whose coordinates are

(X + 1, y), (x-1, y), (x, y + 1), (x, y-1)

This set of pixels, which are called 4-neighbors of p note $N_4(P)$. Each pixel is a unit distance of (x, y).P diagonal neighbors have coordinates

(X + 1, y + 1), (x + 1, y-1), (x-1, y + 1), (x-1, y-1)

and N are noticed $_D(P)$. These points, together with the four neighbors are called eight-neighbors py noticeable $N_8(P)$.

4.2.1.2. Connectivity

The connection between pixels is an important concept used to establish the boundaries of objects and component regions of an image. To determine if two pixels are connected is to be established if adjacent in some way (for example if 4-neighbors are and if their gray levels satisfy some criterion of similarity, for example, be equal). Thus a binary image or with values 0 and 1 two pixels may be 4-connected neighbors and not be unless they have the same value [2].

Let V be the set of values of gray levels used to define the connectivity: for example in binary images, V = {1} or range as V = {33, 34, ..., 50} images levels gray.

Consider three types of connectivity:

1. *4 – Connectivity*. Two pixels p and q are said values V 4 – connected if q belongs $N_4(P)$.
2. *8 – Connectivity*. Two pixels p and q are said values V 8 – connected if q belongs $N_D(P)$.
3. *m – Connectivity*. Two pixels p and q are said values V m – connected

It is valid that:

a. q belongs to $N_4(P)$ or
b. q belongs to $N_D(P)$ and $N_4(P)$ $N_D(P)$ It is empty. (This is the set 4-neighbors p and q values V).

Importantly, the m-connectivity is introduced to eliminate ambiguity in the possible paths which connect two pixels.

It is said that a pixel p is adjacent aq if connected. It is obvious that this concept depends on the type of connectivity used. Two subsets of image S, S_1, and S_2 We say that are adjacent if a pixel is S_1 It is adjacent to one on S_2.

A road pixel p with coordinates (x, y) coordinates with aq (s, t) is a sequence of distinct pixels with coordinates

$(x_0, Y_0), (X_1, Y_1) \ldots (X_n, Y_n)$

where $(x_0, Y_0) = (X, y)$ *and* $(x_n, Y_n) = (S, t)$, where (x_i, Y_i) adjacent to (x_{i-1}, Y_{i-1}) for $1 \leq i \leq n$, n being then the path length. It is obvious that the type of path depends on the type of adjacency used.

If p and q are pixels in a subset S of an image, then p is connected in aq S if there is a path that is connected in pk S.

4.2.2. Types of Images

4.2.2.1. Color Images

They are images composed of four values stored in three planes or arrays of pixels which are defined by color models. The purpose of a color model is a specification of a model of 3-D coordinates and a subspace within that system where each color is represented by a single point. The models used in image processing are RGB, YIQ, and HSI.

In the RGB model, each color appears in its red, green and blue spectral components primary. The model is based on a Cartesian coordinate system. The subspace of interest is the hub shown in Figure 4.4.

The images in the RGB color model are formed by three planes of separate images, each of the primary colors. When introduced into an RGB monitor, the three images are overlaid on the phosphor screen to produce a composite color image. Therefore, the use of RGB model for image processing makes sense when images is expressed in terms of the three color planes. Alternatively, most color cameras used to acquire digital images using RGB [2] format [5].

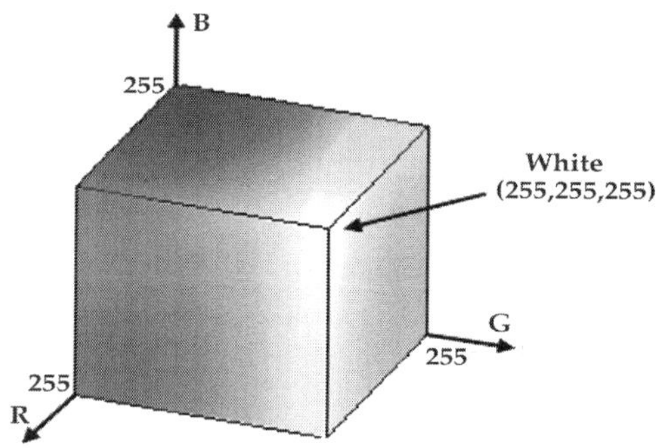

Figure 4.4. RGB color cube, (*Source: self-made or CC-BY license*).

The points on the main diagonal have gray levels from black to white at the origin at the point (1,1,1).

The YIQ model is used in TV broadcasts in color. Basically, YIQ is a re-encoding RGB for transmission efficiency and to maintain compatibility with monochrome TV standards. In fact, the Y component of the YIQ system provides all the video information required for a monochrome television. The RGB to YIQ conversion is given by

$$\begin{pmatrix} Y \\ I \\ Q \end{pmatrix} = \begin{pmatrix} 0,299 & 0,587 & 0,114 \\ 0,596 & -0,275 & -0,321 \\ 0,212 & -0,523 & 0,311 \end{pmatrix} \begin{pmatrix} R \\ G \\ B \end{pmatrix}$$

This system was designed taking into account the characteristics of human visual system, particularly the most sensitive to changes in luminance than to changes of hue or saturation. So, this standard uses more bits (or bandwidth) to represent Y and less for I and Q. In addition to being widely used, one of its major advantages is that the information of luminance (Y) and color (I & Q) are separated. Thus it can be processed without affecting the color luminance [2].

Hue is an attribute that describes the color purity (pure yellow, orange or red), while saturation is the measure of the degree to which a pure color is diluted with white light. HSI utility model is due to two main facts. On the one hand, the current component is separated from the color information plus the other two components are closely related to the way humans perceive color. These features make this model very suitable for the development of processing algorithms based on properties of human vision system [2] images (Figure 4.5).

Figure 4.5. RGB image, (*Source: Self-Made or CC-BY license*).

4.2.2.2. Grayscale Images

They are composite images of a single plane or matrix of pixels, where their values are represented in [0–255] for an 8-bit, where 0 represents the color black and 255 white color, as in that interval all available gray intensities in the image [11] are located (Figure 4.6).

Figure 4.6. Grayscale image, (*Source: self-made or CC-BY license*).

4.2.2.3. Binary Images

They are those where each pixel assumes discrete values of one or zero. These values correspond essentially on or off; where a binary image is stored in a logical order of zeros or off pixels and a pixel or pinned. These are on the border between two different regions, and its detection, an important step for retrieving information [11] (Figure 4.7).

Figure 4.7. Binary image, (*Source: self-made or CC-BY license*).

4.2.3. Pre-Processing

4.2.3.1. Edge Detection

The first steps of the vision try to identify features in the image that are relevant to estimate the structure and properties of objects in the scene. The edges correspond to significant local changes in the image and are probably the most important features for analyzing it.

Simplifying the definition it can be said that an edge is a discontinuity of some kind in the intensity function of the image. But there are many different types of edges, some are due to shadows that occur on objects, others to the change in reflectance of objects or even the texture of objects. As seen in Figure 4.8 the edges are labeled d due to discontinuities between the objects and the camera together with discontinuities in the normal to the object surface. DC labeled discontinuities are due to the distance to the camera but not normal. Labeled n are due to discontinuity in the normal, while the labeled r due to changes in the reflectance of the object, but no change in the geometrical properties.

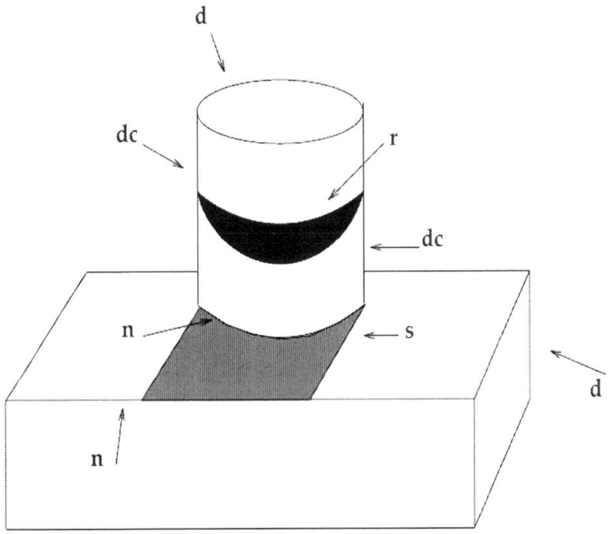

Figure 4.8. Discontinuity in pictures, (*Source: self-made or CC-BY license*).

Such discontinuities are detected using the derived first and second order. The election of the first order derivative image processing is the gradient. The gradient of a function in 2-D, f (x, y) is defined as the vector

$$\nabla F = \begin{bmatrix} G_x \\ G_y \end{bmatrix} = \begin{bmatrix} \dfrac{\partial f}{\partial x} \\ \dfrac{\partial f}{\partial y} \end{bmatrix}$$

The magnitude of this vector is

$$\nabla^2 f = mag(\nabla F) = [G_x^2 + G_y^2]^{-1/2} = \left[\left(\frac{\partial f}{\partial x}\right)^2 + \left(\frac{\partial f}{\partial y}\right)^2\right]^{-1/2}$$

To simplify computationally, this amount is approximately sometimes omitting the square root,

$$\nabla f \approx G_x^2 + G_y^2$$

O using absolute values,

$$\nabla f = |G_x| + |G_y|$$

These approaches still behave as derivatives. For this reason, these approximations are zero in areas of constant intensity and their values are proportional to the degree of intensity change in areas in which the pixel value is variable. There are a lot of detectors borders [2].

Roberts operator is one of the oldest. It is easy to calculate because it uses only a 2x2 window size. Convolution masks are

$$G_x = \begin{bmatrix} 1 & 0 \\ 0 & -1 \end{bmatrix} \qquad G_y = \begin{bmatrix} 0 & 1 \\ -1 & 0 \end{bmatrix}$$

The magnitude of the gradient is calculated by the following approximation

$$G(f(i,j)) = |f(i,j) - f(i+1,j+1)| + |f(i,j+1) - f(i+1,j)|$$

Since G_x and G_Y are approximations of the partial derivatives with respect to x and y, respectively. A disadvantage Roberts operator is that is very sensitive to noise, since they are used very few pixels to approximate the gradient.

One way to avoid that the gradient is calculated at an intermediate point, as occurs in the Roberts operator, is to use 3 x 3 environments. Consider the pixel distribution shown around (i, j) in Figure 2.6.

The Sobel operator is the magnitude of the gradient calculated by

$$M = \sqrt{S_x^2 + S_y^2}$$

Where the partial derivatives are calculated by

$$S_x = (a_2 + ca_3 + a_4) - (a_0 + ca_7 + a_6)$$
$$S_y = (a_0 + ca_1 + a_2) - (a_2 + ca_5 + a_4)$$

With constant c = 2.

Clearly, these operators can implement gradient using convolution masks, which is a form that the function is displayed based on the connectivity of pixels. It is important to note that this operator gives more weight to those closest to the center of the mask pixels. This operator is one of the most used (Figure 4.9).

a_0	a_1	a_2
a_7	(i, j)	a_3
a_6	a_5	a_4

Figure 4.9. Labeling of gray level for explaining the edge detectors, (*Source: self-made or CC-BY license*).

Derived second order in image processing are generally computed using the Laplacian. The Laplacian of a function f 2-D (x, y) is formed by the second order derivatives, as shown below:

$$\nabla^2 f = \partial^2 f / \partial x^2 + \partial^2 f / \partial y^2$$

The second derivative in the x and y directions are approximated using difference equations

$$\partial(f(i+1j) - f(ij))$$

$$\frac{}{\partial x^2} = \frac{G_x}{\partial_x} = \frac{, \quad ,}{\partial_x} = f(i+2, j) - 2f(i+1, j) + f(i, j)$$

Analogously would be obtained

$$\frac{\partial^2 f}{\partial y^2} = f(i, j+2) - 2f(i, j+1) + f(i, j)$$

However, these two approaches are not centered at the position (i, j) so that it would be more reasonable approximation

$$\frac{\partial^2 f}{\partial x^2} = f(i+1, j) - 2f(i, j) + f(i-1, j)$$

$$\frac{\partial^2 f}{\partial y^2} = f(i, j+1) - 2f(i, j) + f(i, j-1)$$

Combining these two equations in a single operator can use the following mask to approximate to Laplacian

$\nabla^2 \approx$

0	1	0
4	-4	1
0	1	0

Sometimes it is desirable to give more weight to the central pixel of the environment.

An approximation of the Laplacian doing this is

$\nabla^2 \approx$

1	4	1
4	-20	4
1	4	1

The Laplacian operator marks the presence of an edge when the operator output makes a zero crossing. The trivial zeros, i.e., regions of uniform zero must be ignored. In principle, the locations of zero crossings can be estimated sub-pixel level using linear interpolation; but the results may not be accurate.

4.2.4. Image Segmentation

The first step in image analysis is generally segment the image into regions. A region in an image, is a group of connected pixels (a concept that needs to be precisely defined) having similar properties. It is obvious that regions are important for the interpretation of the images it may correspond to object in the scene. An image may also contain various objects and each object can contain several regions corresponding to parts thereof [2, 5].

So that an image can be interpreted correctly, it must be divided into regions corresponding to objects or parts thereof. However, due to segmentation errors, correspondence between regions and objects will not be perfect and we use specific knowledge in later stages of image interpretation.

4.2.4.1. Regions and Bordes

The first step in the analysis to understand an image is to partition the image so that regions representing different objects are explicitly marked. These partitions can be obtained from the characteristics of the gray levels in the image, or using another. Thus, one could say that the gray values in the image positions are observations and other attributes, such as belonging to regions should be obtained from the gray levels. There are two approaches for partitioning an image into regions based on regions and frontier estimation using edge detectors [2] segmentation.

In the approach based on regions, all pixels corresponding to an object are grouped together and are marked to indicate that they belong to a region. This process is called segmentation. Pixels are allocated to regions according to some criterion that distinguishes them from the rest of the image. Two very important principles are value segmentation similarity and spatial proximity. Two pixels can be assigned to the same region if they have similar characteristics and intensity if they are close. The variance of the gray levels in one region and the compactification of a region may also be used as similarity values and proximity pixels respectively [2].

Just as in the problem of segmentation similarity between levels, you can also perform this process by what is called disparity. The goal is to find the pixels that are on the borders of the regions. These pixels, called edges, can be located by examining neighboring pixels. Since the pixels are called edges in the border regions and these often have different gray levels on each side, what is needed it is to measure the difference between neighboring pixels. Most edge detectors used only the characteristics of the intensity for detection, although some aspects like texture and movement also provide information.

It is necessary to define what is meant by segmentation. A complete segmentation of an R image is a finite set of regions R_I, ..., R_s such that

$$R = U_{I=1}^{S} R_I \quad R_I \cap R_J = 0 \quad i \neq j$$

Based on thresholding segmentation (Figure 4.10)

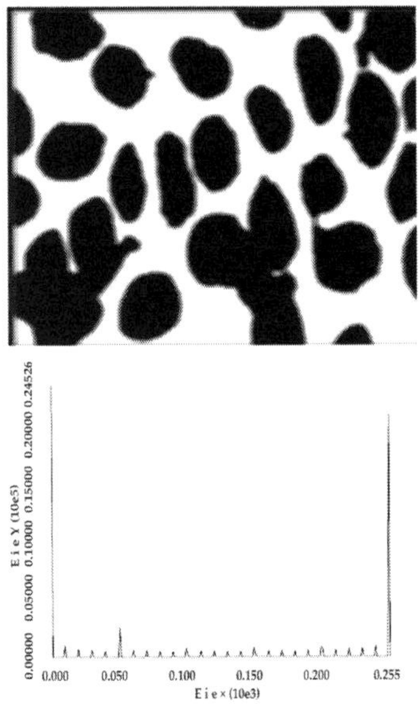

Figure 4.10. Histogram of gray levels, (*Source: self-made or CC-BY license*).

Corresponding to an image f (x, y) composed of dark objects on bright background so that the pixels in objects and background are gray levels grouped into two dominant fashion. An obvious way to extract background objects is to select a threshold T which separates these fashions. That is, write

$$g(i,j)=\begin{cases}1 & si\ \ f(i,j)\geq T\\ 0 & si\ \ f(i,j)<T\end{cases}$$

This equation has many modifications. One possibility is to segment the image into regions of pixels with gray level in a set D and the rest as background. You can also use multiple thresholds, resulting in non-binary images with a very limited set of gray levels, the process would be

$$\begin{aligned} g(i,j) &= 1\ \ si\ \ f(i,j)\in D_1\\ &= 2\ \ si\ \ f(i,j)\in D_2\\ &= 3\ \ si\ \ f(i,j)\in D_3\\ &\dots\\ &= n\ \ si\ \ f(i,j)\in D_n \end{aligned}$$

This type of multilevel thresholding is generally less reliable than thresholding in two regions. The reason is that it is difficult to establish multiple thresholds to isolate regions correctly, especially when there are many fads (local maxima).

It is clear that to make the most robust segmentation, the threshold should be automatically selected by the system, for this work, both knowledge about the scene as the problem to solve and any other knowledge should be used to set the threshold. It can also have the information provided by the characteristics of objects, the size thereof, the fraction of the image occupied by the objects and the different types of objects that can appear in the image [2].

4.2.4.2. Edge-Based Segmentation

Historically the first group of segmentation methods, which is still very important information is based on image edges. Segmentation techniques based on edges found by using the edges the detectors. The ultimate goal is to achieve at least partial segmentation, i.e., grouping local edges in an image where only edges chains with a correspondence with objects in the image or part of the image are present.

There are different methods for segmentation based on edges that differ in the strategy for building border as well as in the amount of prior information is incorporated into the method. It is obvious that more information to better segmentation.

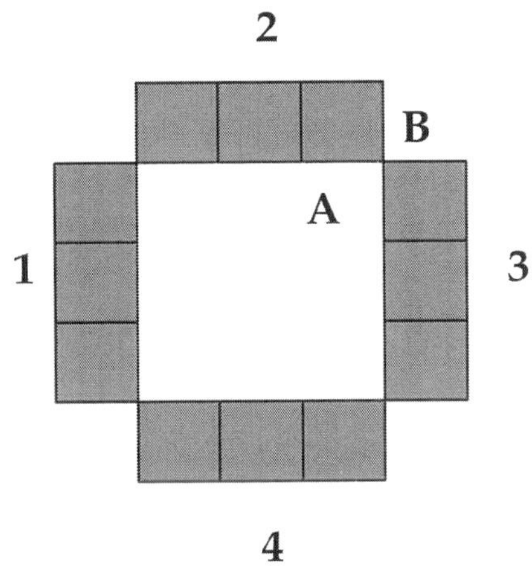

Figure 4.11. Problems with connectivity, (*Source: self-made or CC-BY license*).

Borders are joined edges that characterize the shape of an object. They are therefore useful for calculating geometric features such as size and orientation. Conceptually, the borders can be found by tracing the edges connected (either 4 or 8 connected). However, there are difficulties associated with these definitions of connectivity, as shown in Figure 4.12. If we use the 4-connectivity segments 1, 2, 3 and 4 would be classified as disjoint, although clearly seem to form a ring. Under the 8-connectivity these segments would be connected, but so would the inside to the outside of the ring. In principle, this could be solved by using different types of connectivity for objects and the background.

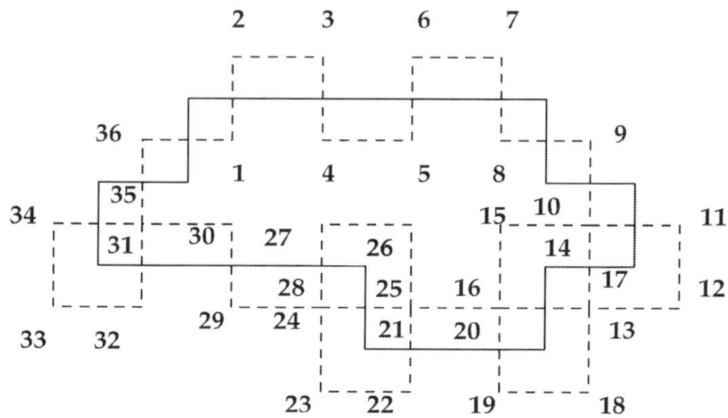

Figure 4.12. Contour follow, (*Source: self-made or CC-BY license*).

Moreover, tracking algorithms contour tracing borders ordering successive points edge type. An algorithm to trace closed borders in binary images is as follows:

1. Start within the region A, (for example, the first pixel found in the region when we make a tracking rows),
2. Turn left and go to the next pixel if we are within the region A, otherwise turn right and pass the next pixel,
3. You continue until you reach the point from which departed.

Figure 4.12 shows an example of how an outline is followed. In the image, it looks like when walking the edges must take into account the points where it enters and leaves the region.

4.2.4.3. *Segmenting Oriented Regions*

The most natural method for growing regions is to begin considering each pixel of the image as a region obviously in this case each region is homogeneous, but may not necessarily meet the criterion of being the highest regions, the process must be repeated until regions are maximal. In algorithm, the method would be:

1. Define an initial segmentation that meets the criterion of homogeneity,
2. Defining criteria for joining adjacent regions,
3. Join adjacent regions if they meet the criteria binding. Stop when you cannot join two regions without breaking the homogeneity criterion.

0	0	5	6	7
1	1	5	8	7
0	1	5	6	7
2	0	7	6	6
0	1	5	6	5

(a)

a	a	b	b	b
a	a	b	b	b
a	a	b	b	b
a	a	b	b	b
a	a	b	b	b

(b)

a	a	a	a	a
a	a	a	a	a
a	a	a	a	a
a	a	a	a	a
a	a	a	a	a

(c)

Figure 4.13. Example region growing from seed points, (*Source: self-made or CC-BY license*).

The simplest implementation of this algorithm begins with the union of regions starting with regions segmentation 2x2, 4x4 or 8x8. Descriptions of the regions is then based on statistical properties of the gray levels, such as in the histogram, the description of a region compared to the other adjacent regions if they match together and the new descriptor of the region is computed. Otherwise, regions are marked that cannot bind [2]. The process continues.

Overall arguably the most important thing is to select the criteria for joining because in this way is possible to obtain better segmentation with which it will work. A heuristic criteria type used in order to provide good bonding of pixels of a region is joining two regions R_i and R_j if $w/P_m > \theta_1$ where $P_m = \text{Min}(P_i, P_j)$ P_i and p_j. They are perimeters R_i and R_j and W is the number of locations of weak borders (pixels in which the difference is less than a certain threshold).

The region growing method is a grouping pixels or subregions in larger regions. The simplest form of this process is called aggregation of pixels that begins with a set of pixels seed and from them grows the region adding to said seed pixel neighbors who have similar properties (gray level, color, texture).

To illustrate this procedure can be considered Figure 2.10, where the numbers into the cells represent gray levels. Let the coordinate points (3,2) and (3,4) located in the matrix (a) and underlined therein, the seeds being considered. If these two points are used seeds have a segmentation consists of two regions as: a region R_1 associated with the seed (3.2) and another R_2 associated with (3.4). Property P which will be used to include a pixel in a region is that the difference in absolute value between the gray levels and seed pixel are smaller than a threshold T. Any pixel that meets the given property with respect to the two pixels it is arbitrarily assigned to one of the regions. Figure 2.10 (b) shows the result of T=3. The two segmented regions are noted and b. with T = 8 would a single segmentation as shown in 02/10 (c).

4.2.5. Morphological Image Processing

The no morphological approach images this next calculation, based on concepts such as the Dirac delta, PSF, and linear transformations as convolution, however, mathematical morphology is based primarily on the geometry and shape, morphological operations simplify images and retain the main features of shapes of objects.

A system operators such as mathematical morphology is useful because it can form compositions of the operators, which when acting on complex shapes, are able to break them down into parts that make sense and separate parts that are foreign. A system of this type operators and composition allows the underlying forms are identified and optimally reconstructed from their distorted and noisy forms. It also allows each form to be understood in terms of a decomposition, each entity of a simple decomposition appropriate [2, 5].

Morphological changes usually are an intermediate part of the sequence of image processing, then a summary of which is presented are the processing steps:

In the first stage, the image is digitized and preprocessed using convolution operators local then is segmented to obtain a binary image in which the background objects are separated.

1. Morphological operations can form a second phase which operates on the shape of these objects.
2. The last processing step evaluates the results of the morphology using numerical or syntactic descriptors.

Mathematical morphology can be used, among others, the following objectives:

1. Pre-processing (noise suppression, simplified forms),
2. Highlight the structure of objects (extract the skeleton, marking objects, convex hull, enlargement, reduction),
3. Qualitative description of objects (area, perimeter, etc.).

The language of binary mathematical morphology is based on set theory, therefore it is necessary to know some basics of basic operations on sets.

4.2.6. Basic Operations on Sets

Let A and B sets in n-space E^n elements a = $(a_1, \ldots, to_n)$ b = $(b_1, \ldots, b_n)$ respectively both tuples being.

Lemma 1. By xAND^n Note that A_x is defined as

$$TO_x = \{C \mid c = a + x, \text{for some } A \qquad TO\}$$

The reflection *B* notated B ^ is defined as

$$B \wedge = \{x \mid x = -b, b \qquad B\}$$

The difference of two sets A and B, notated A – B, it is defined by

$$A - B = \{x \mid xA, x \qquad B\}$$

4.2.7. Binary morphology

As previously said, the language of binary mathematical morphology is based on set theory. Sets in mathematical morphology represent the forms present in binary or gray level images. The set of all the white pixels of an image in black and white (binary) is a complete description of the image.

Points in a set on which the transformation is applied are the set of selected points and a complementary unselected. In binary images selected points are those who do not belong to the fund.

Morphological operations are primary erosion and dilation. Dilation is morphological transformation that combines two vectors using the sum. The binary dilation was first used by Minkowski, and in the mathematical literature called the Minkowski sum. If A and B are set in n-space E^n elements a = (a_1, ..., to_n) b = (b_1, ..., b_n) both tuples, then dilating A by B is the set of all possible vectors is the sum of pairs of elements, one of A and B respectively being other (Figure 4.14).

More formally, dilation of A by B note A ⊕ *B* and it is defined by

$$A\oplus B = \{c \in \quad \oplus \quad ANDn \mid C = a + b \text{ for some to} + \quad A\, b \in B\}$$

As commutative sum, it is also dilation: A

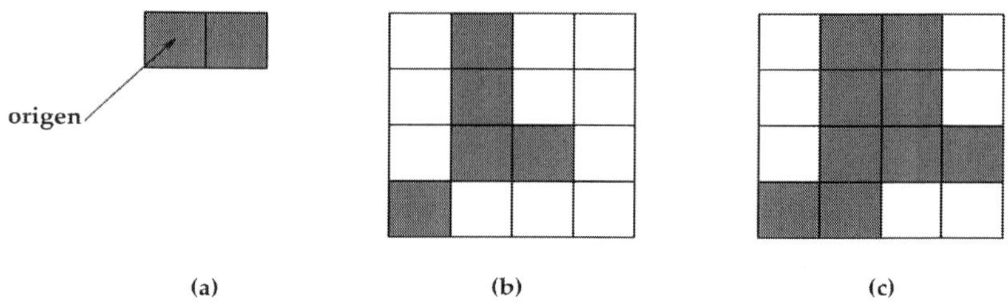

Figure 4.14. Example dilation, (*Source: self-made or CC-BY license*).

⊕ In practice sets A and B are not symmetrical. The first element of expansion, A, is associated with the image being processed and the second is called structural element, the shape acting on the dilating A to produce A-B.

When a dilation with a structural element-containing zero is performed, which it makes it the expansion of an image and is easy to think of a parallel implementation. An example is shown in Figure 2.11, where the row across the image, to find a black pixel, one to the right of it is added. It is important to note that the coordinate system to be used in this topic is (row, column).

Dilation has the following properties

- Dilation by the transfer of a structural element is the transfer of dilation:

$$A\oplus B_i = (A\oplus B)_i$$

- Distributive property:

$$A\oplus(B \cup C) = (A\oplus B) \cup (A\oplus C)$$

- Associativity (iteration):

$$A\oplus(B\oplus C) = (A\oplus B)\oplus C$$

Erosion is the dual morphological operation, a concept which is formally defined from dilation. Is the morphological transformation that combines two sets using the concept of inclusion. If A and B are set in the n-dimensional Euclidean space, then erosion A by B is the set of all elements for which x x + b A b for all B. Minkowski subtraction is closely related to erosion [2] (Figure 4.15).

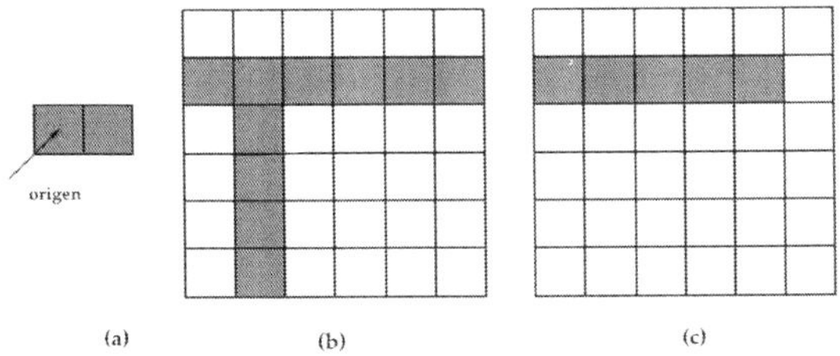

Figure 4.15. Example erosion, (*Source: self-made or CC-BY license*).

The erosion of A by B is noted A $\ominus$ *B* and its definition is

$$A \ominus B = \{x \quad AND^{n}|x + bA \text{ for all } b\in B\}$$

An example of erosion in Figure 2.12, finding a black pixel is checked if the right side is accompanied by another black pixel, if the pixel as this is allowed, otherwise, it is replaced by a white pixel.

The usefulness of erosion can be better appreciated when it is expressed differently. The erosion of an image, A, by a structural element, B, is the set of all elements x E^n for which B moved by x is contained in A demonstration is immediate and must.

$$A \ominus B = \{xE\in \quad ^{n}| B_{x} \quad A\}$$

While the expansion can be represented as the union of shipments, erosion can be represented as the intersection of the negative transfers.

$$A \ominus B = \quad _{b} \quad _{B}A_{-b}$$

Erosion is usually seen as a reduction of the original image. In terms of set theory, the whole is often eroded think that is always contained in the original.

4.2.8. Feature Extraction

Once an image has been segmented into regions by the methods discussed in the above issues, it is necessary to represent and describe these pixels so that they can be processed later. Arguably, there are two options

1. Represent a region depending on its border.
2. Make representation according to their internal characteristics.

Once you have chosen the representation has to find a way to describe it. For example, you can choose a representation based on the boundary and describe by its length, the number of concavities having, etc (Figure 4.16).

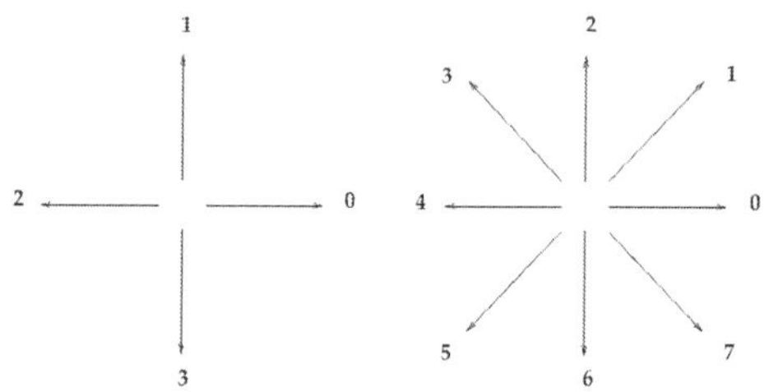

Figure 4.16. Addresses used to classify the border, (*Source: self-made or CC-BY license*).

4.2.9. Representation of the Border

Representation based on the border is more used when the emphasis is on the way. Representation based on the border is used more when properties such as color or texture are sought. In any case, the features that are selected as descriptors must be insensitive to changes as variations in size, translation, rotation, etc.

The code strings are used to represent borders a connected series of straight line segments and a length given direction. Normally this representation is based on the 4- or 8-connectivity. The address of each segment is encoded using a numbering scheme as shown in Figure 4.16, in the first figure can only build a string horizontal codes and vertically which would cause a less detailed description of the object while the second It shows that the chain can be constructed taking into account the diagonal paths [2].

Figure 4.17 shows an example of representation of a border using code strings. Obviously, the code string depends on the starting point and normalization for future comparison is necessary.

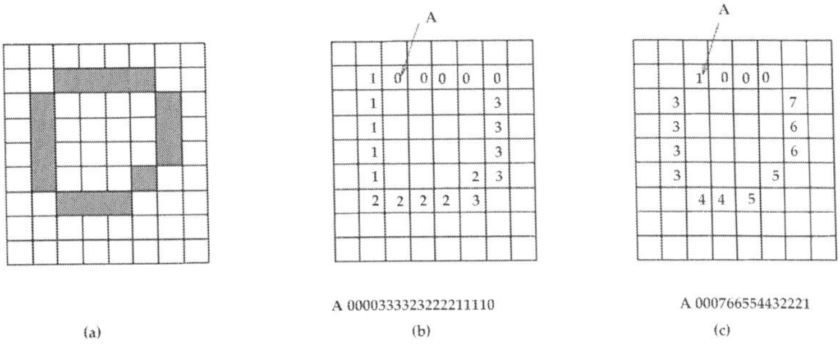

(a) border, (b) 4-connectivity, (c) 8-connectivity

Figure 4.17. Encodings border, (*Source: self-made or CC-BY license*).

A digital frontier can be approximated by a polygon. If the curve is closed, the approximation is accurate when the number of segments in the polygon match the number of border points, so that each pair of adjacent points defines a segment of the polygon. In practice, the object of a polygonal approximation is to capture the essence of the shape of the border with the smallest possible number of polygonal segments. The problem is not trivial and may require enormous computing power. However, several techniques are polygonal approximation at the same time simple and good [2].

An approach frequently used subdivides a segment successively into two parts until a certain criterion is satisfied. *For example*, it may require that the maximum perpendicular distance from one boundary segment to the line connecting the two endpoints does not exceed a given threshold. If exceeds the threshold, the farthest point becomes vertex and divides the segment into two sub-segments. This approach has the advantage that seeks prominent turning points. The example illustrated in Figure 4.18.

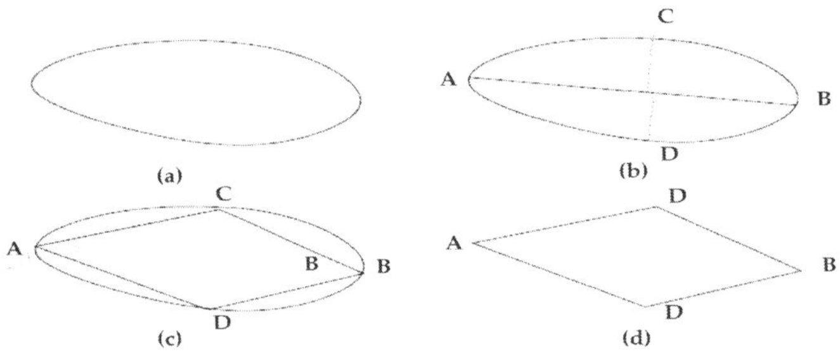

Figure 4.18. A polygonal approximations border, (*Source: self-made or CC-BY license*).

4.2.10. Representation of the Regions

The shape of an object can be represented directly by the region it occupies. For example the binary matrix

$$u(m,n) = 1, if\ (m,n) \in R$$

$$u(m,n) = 0, if\ not\,(m,n) \in R$$

It is a representation of the R region, although obviously, the boundary representation is more efficient than this procedure.

Any region or variable image can be viewed as a sequence in which rows of zeros and ones alternate. The variable length codes representing these rows. For an image is scanned by rows up to the region of interest, the code is the start address of each row followed by the number of ones or zeros within it.

In the method of quad-trees, the given region is included in a rectangular area convenient. This area is divided into four quadrants and examined each to see if all its pixels belong to the same region or not. If you have within and outside the region, it follows subdividing. Arbole structure is generated until each quadrant sub-pixel contains only one type. Assuming used 1 for the region and 0 for nonregion, then the tree can be coded uniquely as a string of zeros, ones and gray to denote noncoding region, region and necessary subdivision [2], see Figure 4.19.

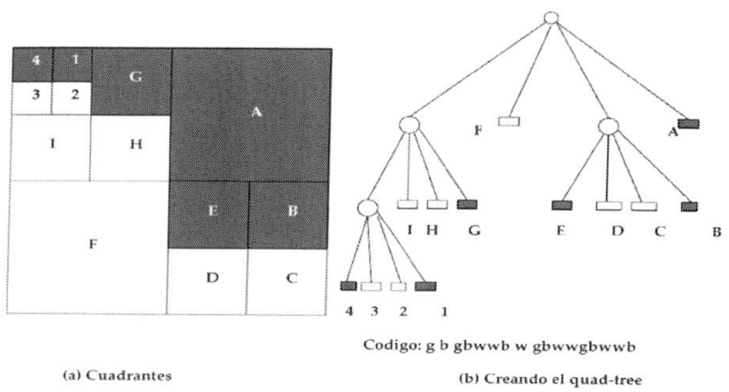

Figure 4.19. Example of quad-trees method, (*Source: self-made or CC-BY license*).

4.3. APPLYING NEURAL NETWORKS

4.3.1. The Artificial Neuron

The first Neural Network by McCulloch and Pitts made in 1943, was an electrical circuit performing the weighted sum of different binary signals and binary output according to the result of the sum relative to the threshold. A good representation of what is an artificial neuron is based on the parameters shown below [10].

- Inputs: x1, x2, ..., Xn. Each entry is attached a weight w1, w2, ..., Wn; an input to the neuron, called bias, has a constant value of 1 and is usually represented as a separate entry, but for simplicity treated as a normal input constant value.
- An excitation function f, which generally calculates the sum of each entry is assigned the weight u
- An activation function that calculates the level s activation of a neuron = s (u).

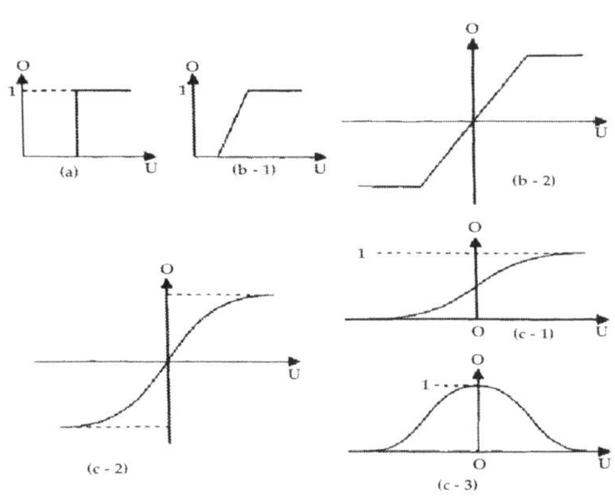

Figure 4.20. Activation features, (*Source: self-made or CC-BY license*).

A transfer function that calculates the value to be sent by the output (axon) of a neuron or = g (a); usually the output is assumed equal to the activation level of the neuron, or = to.

Depending on the kind of values that each parameter may have each different type of neuron, the input and output can be binary, {0, 1}; Bivalent, {- 1, 1}; continuous, [0, 1]; or discrete numbers in a defined interval [10].

Activation functions most frequently used are shown in the figure are:

1. The unit step function threshold. If the value of the sum or of the neuron is above the threshold, the neuron becomes exciter (activation value of 1); but becomes inhibitory (activation value of 0).
2. Linear threshold function. The trigger value increases linearly with the u value, but when the output reaches a threshold saturates (value of 1); but there are different variable range this function depending on the need to take the output of the neuron. (Figure 2.17 [b–1] and [b–2]).
3. Sigmoid function. It is a non-linear transformation function S-shaped characterized by the following:

A. Have their restricted between two points, for example, values [0, 1], [–1, 1].

B. The value of s (u) never decreases even though u increase.

C. Continuous and smooth, therefore differentiable at any point in the domain. Different types of sinusoidal functions are used in practice. Most of them are the logistic function: a = $1/(1 + e^{-or})$. More generally the logistic function can be written as: a = $1/(1 + e^{-c \cdot u})$, with c as constant.

D. There are alternatives to this function such as bipolar logistics: $h(u) = (1 - e^{-or})/(1 + e^{-or}) = 2g(u) - 1$; this function has a range of [–1, 1] and the hyperbolic tangent: tanh (u) = $(e^{or} - e^{-or})/(and^{or} + e^{-or})$.

4. The Gaussian function (bell-shaped) (Figure 2.17 [c–3]).

An output neuron could be represented by a single static potential or a pulse, which can occur (coded as 1) or not (encoded as 0).

Although a single neuron is able to perform some simple function, it is at the junction of several neurons that can solve a lot of complex problems.

4.3.2. Artificial Neural Network

Usually, an artificial Neural Network is modeled computationally by four parameters:

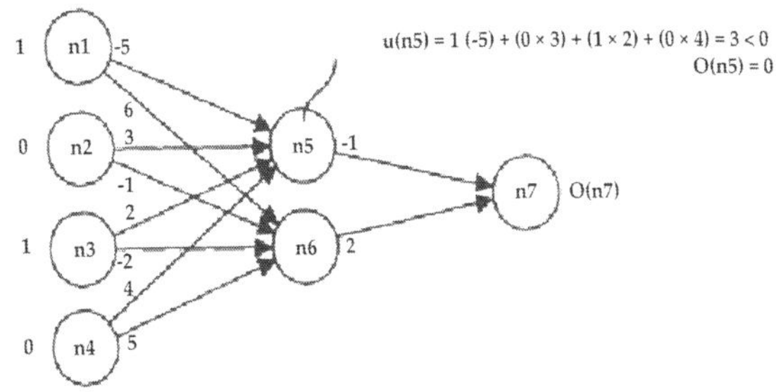

Figure 4.21. Example Neural Network, (*Source: self-made or CC-BY license*).

1. Type of neurons (also known as nodes).
2. The organization of connections between neurons.
3. Training algorithm.
4. Algorithm memory.

In a Neural Network, the manner in which neurons are connected defined topology, neurons may be fully connected, where each neuron is connected to each of the other neurons or partially connected, for example, when only connections allowed between neurons in different layers or in general not all possible connections between neurons are connected [10].

Depending on the presence or absence of feedback in the Neural Network,

Two types of architectures are distinguished:

1. Feedforward architecture. No output connections of the Neural Network to the input; these networks bear no memory of their previous state, the next state depends only on new entries, Perceptron networks are an example.
2. Feedback architecture. There are output connections of the Neural Network to the input; such networks memory stored previous state, the next state depends not only on new entries but also the previous state, Hopfield networks are an example of such networks.

The greatest feature of Neural Networks is their ability to learn, this makes it possible behavior modification in response to the environment. A Neural Network is trained for then to enter an input vector X a desired output (or at least consistent) of a vector Y, or the network to learn about the internal characteristics and data structures of an input vector X to occur.

The set X, used to train the network is called the training set, the elements of the set x X are called training examples. The training process is reflected in changing weights between connections of different neurons. During training, the Neural Network is gradually converging to values such that each training vector x, the network produces the desired output.

The ability to learn from one neuron is achieved through the use of a learning algorithm. Training algorithms can be largely classified into the following three groups:

1. Supervised: For supervised training vectors has both input and output training is achieved when the network associated with each of the input vectors into a desired output.
2. Unsupervised: You are only supplied to the grid is the input vector, the Neural Network learns some features of the whole input it is presented.
3. Reinforcement learning: Sometimes called learning reward and punishment is a combination of the above two paradigms; It is based on presenting an input vector x to the Neural Network and looking in output vector calculated by network. If it is considered "good" it is given a "reward" in the sense that the connections, otherwise, the network is "punished" reinforcing, connections "are considered appropriate" are inhibited. In this way, the reinforcement learning is learning with a critical and not a teacher.

Learning is not a skill one neuron. It is a collective process of entire Neural Network and is as a result of a learning activity. The weight matrix W has meaning as an overall pattern, and it represents "knowledge." Although you really do not know the way in which the brain learns. In artificial Neural Networks, it has reached a learning genetic laws [10].

The law currently learning more favored in the connectionist model law Hebbian learning, the idea is that synaptic connection between two neurons i and j increases its connection w_{ij} if the two neurons i and j are simultaneously activated repeatedly by a stimulus. Change ∇ synaptic weight *wij* is calculated as the function then the product of two values activation $_i$ and a_j iyj of neurons:

$$\nabla wij = C * ai*aj$$

The general process of learning in a Neural Network is described by a feature called convergence. The network reacts increasingly better xa input as more vectors are introduced into the Neural Network and ultimately leading to the expected response. After the training is completed the weights do not change more, that's *wij*= 0, for each connection (i, j) when new data or examples thereof are then entered to the network. The network can be trained for the two reasons: (1) the network has learned the examples, and (2) the network is saturated.

Theorem Grossberg saturation indicates that large input signals saturates when a neuron is sensitive to small input signals, but is sensitive to large inputs, small inputs are ignored as noise [10].

$wij = C * ai*aj+ n,$

where, n is the noise signal.

When noise occurs during training, the Neural Network reaches a convergence when the weights change according to the magnitude of the noise (stochastic equilibrium).

$wij \leq n$

The state of convergence can also be reached in an oscillatory manner, which means that the synaptic weights ranging between two or more states.

X_1 = Training input

X'= New Entry

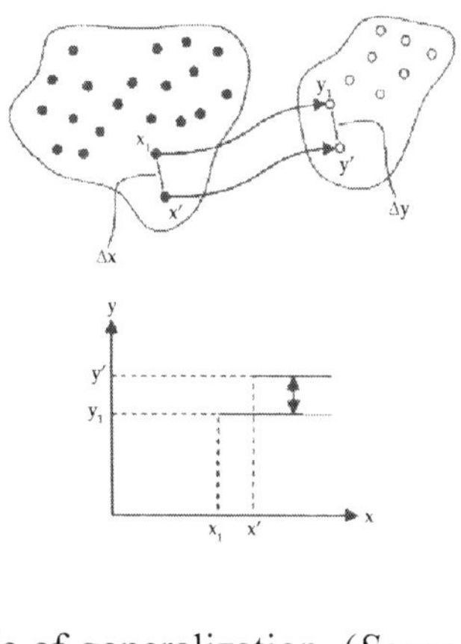

Figure 4.22. The principle of generalization, (*Source: self-made or CC-BY license*).

Another general feature of Neural Networks, similar to the ability of the human brain, is the generalization. This happens when, after training the Neural Network, a new input vector x is presented to the network and a memory function is activated. The network must produce a similar training sort, i.e., out if the new entry is similar to one of the inputs of training.

The general principle is that a similar stimulus should produce a similar response. Figure 4.21 shows graphically as a Neural Network generalizes a new entry.

Generalizing could take a lot of iterations of consecutive calculations of network conditions, which is the case for recurrent networks. Eventually, the network reaches a steady state, when the network does not change their status to move to a next iteration, as if froze in that state. This phenomenon is seen in Hopfield networks. It is analogous to the process of trying to associate a face with one that has been seen in the past, in order to remember where we have seen the person who greeted us at a party.

4.3.3. Supervised Training

Supervised training is mainly based on having a history to determine how entries must be properly mapped to the exits. So that the supervised training can be seen as a relationship between a domain space and a solution space problem: X -> Y, where samples (examples) of the pair (input vector, output vector); (X, y) are known, x X, and Y, x = (x1, x2,..., Xn) and y = (yl, y2,..., M). How to approximate F 'tagged data using Neural Networks widespread enough to give a satisfactory response to new inputs is the problem concerning the supervised training. Usually, this type of training usually uses the following sequence:

1. Organize an appropriate structure for the Neural Network, having, for example, (n + 1) input neurons (n by the input variable and the bias 1, x_0) And m output neurons after selecting a network for the entire initial weights.
2. Enter the network a vector x of the training set.
3. Calculate the output vector or produced by the Neural Network.
4. Compare the vector or the desired vector. If possible, evaluate the error.
5. Correct the weight of the connection so that the next time an input vector x is presented to the network, the output produced is a little closer to the desired output.
6. If necessary, repeat step 2 through 5 until the network reaches a state of convergence.

Evaluate the error is an important part of this training, this evaluation can be done in different ways, and the most used are the instantaneous error: $err = (o - y), o\, err = | o - y |$

The mean square error (MSE):

$$err = \frac{(o - y)^2}{2}$$

Total sum of squared errors overall individual examples and all the output neurons of the network:

$$err = \frac{\left(\sum_{k=1}^{p} \sum_{j=1}^{m} (o_j^{(k)} - oy_j^{(k)})^2\right)}{p * m}$$

where depending on how the error is calculated, two types of errors can be evaluated in a Neural Network. The first, called the apparent error, estimated well a trained network approaches to training examples. The second, called the test error estimates how well a trained network can generalize this means, successfully react to new entries [10].

Different algorithms of supervised training, even though in principle they all have the same bases, the main difference lies in the way in which the weights of the connections are changed through training. Some of these algorithms are training perceptron (Rosenblatt 1958 [28]); ADALINE (Widrow and Hoff 1960 [29]); and backpropagation algorithm (Rumelhart et al., 1995 [30]) .

4.3.4. The Perceptron

The perceptron, which was initially proposed by Rosenblatt (1958) [28], as a single neuron that is used to classify an input from one or two linearly distinguishable categories. You can have multiple entries that are arranged in a grid. This organization can be used to represent an image, or a field of view, and that is why the perceptron can be used to achieve a simple image classification or recognition tasks [10]. Perceptron basic design can be seen in Figure 4.23.

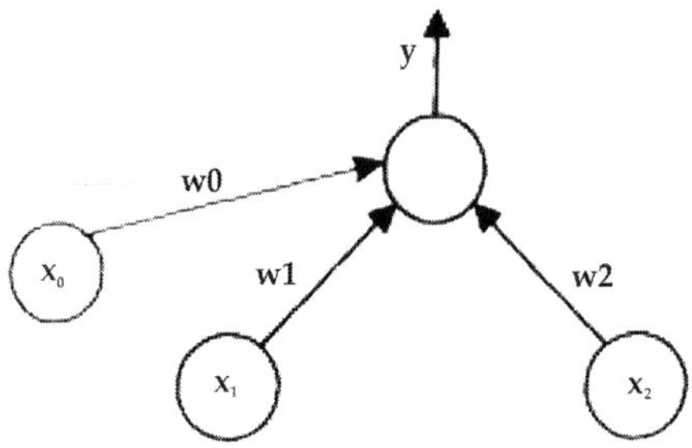

Figure 4.23. A simple perceptron, (*Source: self-made or CC-BY license*).

The perceptron training is achieved when misclassified an entry, then weights so that if a 1 output is desired and the value produced by the network is 0, the value of the weights increases or decreases in the opposite case are changed. If the value produced at the output or $_{j\,(k)}$ It is equal to the desired value and $_{j\,(k)}$ the values of the weights do not change. Following are the general steps perceptron training algorithm:

P1. Organize a perceptron with (n + 1) inputs and m outputs. All weights between connections w_{ij}, I = 1, 2, ..., n and j = 1, 2, ..., m; small values random.

P2. Entering the network a vector x of training set X and calculate the excitation function u_j for each output neuron j using the formula:

$$u_j = \sum (x_j * w_{ij})$$

for i = 1, 2, ..., n and j = 1, 2, ..., m where x_0 is the bias.

P3. Apply a threshold function unit step to the result of the excitation function, as follows:

$or_j = 1$ if $u_j >$ Threshold, but $or_j = 0$.

P4. Calculate the error for each neuron by comparing the current value of the desired output:

$$\_y).$$

$$Err = (0$$

P5. Modify each weight w_{ij} when calculating the new value $w_{ij}(T + 1)$ based on the previous $w_{ij}(T)$ and evaluated the error Err_j:

$$*Err\ ,$$

$$w_{ij}(t+1) = w_{ij}(t) + \alpha x_i \quad j$$

where, the learning coefficient, a number between 0 and 1.

P6. Repeat step between P2 and P5 until the error is small enough.

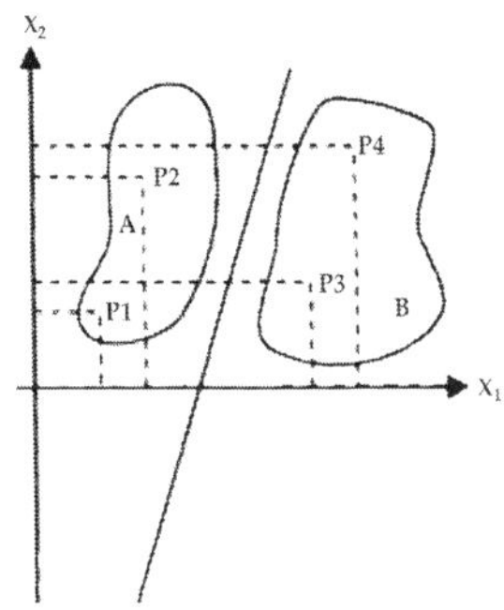

Figure 4.24. Example two linearly separable classes, (*Source: self-made or CC-BY license*).

As shown in Figure 4.24 perceptron can only classify linearly separable classes, as shown in Figure 4.25, such separation can be used to solve the OR function, but presents problems when separated XOR.

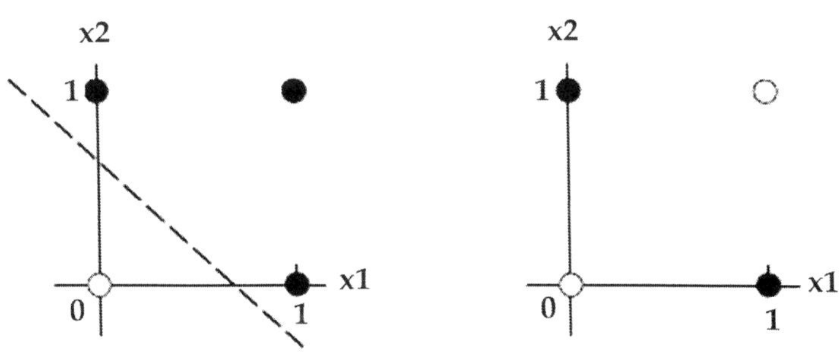

Figure 4.25. XOR problem, (*Source: self-made or CC-BY license*).

The reason why a single perceptron can only model that are linearly separable functions can be seen by reviewing the transfer function of this type of neuron.

$$X = \sum_{i=1}^{n} x_i * w_i$$

$$Y = 1, if\ X \geq threshold$$

$$Y = 0, if\ X < threshold$$

Using these functions, it is successfully dividing the search space using a line in which X = threshold. Thus, a perceptron with two inputs, the line dividing the other class is defined by

$$w_1 x_1 + w_2 x_2 = umbral$$

Given the above note how the perceptron works it is simple, despite this; it still is widely used for its simple architecture and unconditional convergence when considering linearly separable classes. But for more complex problems you need to use other networks that can achieve nonlinear separations and multiple classifiers.

4.3.5. Multilayer Neural Networks and Backpropagation Algorithm

Most problems in the real world are not linearly separable, it is for this reason that even though the perceptron is a good study model to understand how Neural Networks work, but to work on real problems need something that can work with nonlinear systems. As described above Neural Networks consist of a number of connected neurons, usually arranged in layers.

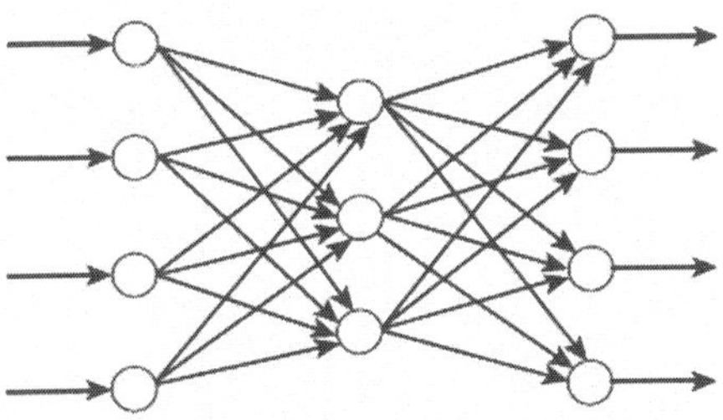

Figure 4.26. Example Neural Network feed-forward, (*Source: self-made or CC-BY license*).

A single perceptron can be thought of as a layer perceptron. Perceptrons multilayer connected are able to model more complex functions, including those that are not linearly separable as the XOR function.

As seen in Figure 2.22, where an example of a Neural Network feed-forward consisting of three layers shown. The first layer, the input layer. Each node (neuron) receives a signal. In fact, in some cases, these first nodes are not neurons, but simply let through the entrances to the next layer, in this case, the hidden layer. It is normal that a Neural Network has more than one hidden layer, which is usually where the real work is done. Eventually, it is passing the last layer, the output layer. This is responsible for sending the output signal. It is very important to note that the neurons of a layer may be completely or partially connected to neurons in the next layer, depending on the type of problem being treated [7].

The multilayer Neural Networks learn similarly a perceptron. The biggest difference is that each neuron has associated to each input weight, generating a greater amount of weights to adjust when an error. Clearly, the most important question is how to select weights that contribute most to the error. A fairly used method is the backpropagation algorithm.

Instead of using the unit step function, backpropagation Neural Networks often use the sigmoid function shown in Figure 4.1 (c-1). This function is defined as:

$$\sigma(x) = \frac{1}{1+e^{-x}}$$

It is used because it is very easy to differentiate:

$$\frac{d\sigma(x)}{dx} = \sigma(x) * (1-\sigma(x))$$

In the same way, you start training perceptron, backpropagation algorithm begins by initializing the network weights with random values, which are generally small values; in the range [-0.5, 0.5].

And training perceptron, backpropagation algorithm each iteration involves first feed network inputs and observe the answers. In the next phase, which gives the name to the algorithm, which involves looking at how the error propagates from the output layer to the input layer. These values mistake retro act through the network by generating changes in the value of the weights in all neurons. This algorithm is repeated until the outputs of the Neural Network are sufficiently close to the desired values, in other words, until the error is small enough [7].

As the sigmoid function cannot attain the values of 0 or 1, as usual, values for 0.9 and 0.1 1 to 0 are accepted.

Now you should see the formula that is used to adjust the weights in this algorithm. Consider a Neural Network with three layers, i represents the neurons of the input layer, j represents the neurons in the hidden layer, and k represents neurons of the output layer. Thus, w_{ij} It refers to the weights of a connection between a neuron of the input layer and a neuron in the hidden layer.

The function is used to derive an output value for a node j it is:

$$X_j = \sum_{i=1}^{n} x_i * w_{ij} - \theta_j$$

$$Y_j = \frac{1}{1+e^{-x_j}}$$

Where n is the number of inputs from node j; w_{ij} is the weight between node i and node j; θ is the threshold value that is used to node j, which is a random value between 0 and 1; x_i is the input value for the i node; yy_j is the output value produced by the j node.

Once each network node is generating an output, the gradient of the error is calculated for each node k in the output layer. The error signal k is known as the difference between the desired value d_k and the current value for that node y_k.

$$e_k = d_k - y_k$$

The gradient of the error for the output of node k is defined as the error value for node k by the derivative of the activation function:

$$\delta_k = \frac{\partial y_k}{\partial x_k} * e_k$$

x_k is the weighted sum of the input values of node k.

Because and is defined as a sigmoid function of x, it can be used the formula was given above to derive the sigmoid function to obtain the following formula for the gradient error:

$$\delta_k = y_k * (1 - y_k) * e_k$$

Similarly, a gradient error for each node j is calculated in the hidden layer, as shown below:

$$\delta_j = y_j * (1 - y_j) * \sum_{k=1}^{n} w_{ik} * \delta_k$$

Where n is the number of nodes in the output layer, and thus the number of outputs for each node in the hidden layer. Now each network weight, w_{ij} OW_{jk}. It is updated according to the following formula:

$$w_{ij} \leftarrow w_{ij} + \alpha * x_i * \delta_j$$

$$w_{jk} \leftarrow w_{jk} + \alpha * y_j * \delta_k$$

where, x_i is the input value of the node i, and α is the learning rate, which is a positive number below 1, which should not be very high [7].

This method is known as a descendant gradient, that means following the steep path down the surface representing the error function to find the slightest error in space, representing the set of weights that offers the best network performance. In fact, iterations usually end at the time when the sum of squared errors of the output values for all training data at any given time is less than some threshold.

Note that since this method assigns an individual punishment for each of the network nodes by associating weights attached to each node with the error associated with such nodes. In the case of nodes in the hidden layer, no error value for those nodes because it is not known what the desired value. In this case, the weights of each connection between the hidden layer and the output layer. They are multiplied by the error of the output node so that this is distributed among the nodes of the hidden layer according to the percentage by which each node contributes error [7].

5 CHAPTER

IMAGE ANALYSIS SYSTEM

CONTENTS

This chapter will show you how the structure of the system to be developed and the reasons why different algorithms to be used in the creation of it were chosen to explain.

5.1. SYSTEM STRUCTURE

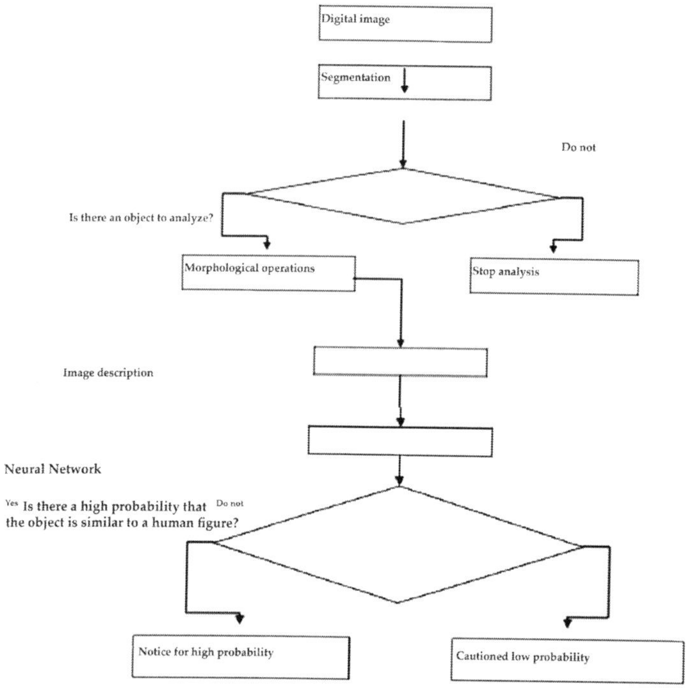

Figure 5.1. System structure, (*Source: self-made or CC-BY license*).

5.2. ANALYSIS OF THE IMAGE

5.2.1. Digital Image

When dealing with similar types of systems it is necessary to choose what kind of image you want to work because they make a good decision could facilitate the rest of the process necessary to analyze the image.

First of all, you should think about the standards that are used by the photographic and common market video equipment, taking this as a starting point quickly noticed that the most common types of images on any device are RGB images and grayscale images.

And at this point, the decision to take is based on the ease with which each type of images allowed to work. RGB images represent very well the objects and their real colors, but is problematic segment the image to have a lot of colors (16,777,256) to review. The images represent grayscale image with 256 colors which makes analyzing these images is easier than with RGB images; In addition, there are a lot of algorithms that allows an image from RGB format to obtain a grayscale.

5.2.2. Segmentation

It is necessary to analyze an image distinguish between the object on which it will work and background image, this process as seen in the previous chapter is known as segmentation. This is possibly the most important part of the analysis of an image.

To make this decision simply what you thought of it easier to implement and can provide acceptable performance; For these reasons, it was thought in the pixel by pixel comparison between two images, one containing only the background and one with the background and image analyzed. Failures such as noise option and problems with extreme changes in lighting known, but it is treatable with a good image capture.

5.2.3. Description of the Image

As seen in the previous chapter, you should find a way to describe the image according to what you want to identify it. For this reason, it has decided to work with the outline of the image as this fits acceptably with the solution to the problem you wish to propose this project, and then represent the outline using a code string.

For the outline of the image have been proposed various algorithms such as it was discussed in the previous chapter, most of them based on either the first or second derivative; when confronted with this decision we chose the one whose implementation was easily found on the network, Sobel algorithm that has been used successfully in various projects. If extraction is successful border will proceed to represent it by a string of codes and then working on it a vector will be used by the Neural Network is created.

First of all, based on the specifications of the problem you come to the conclusion that you should use a Neural Network with supervised training. It is easy to dismiss the use of a perceptron in this system since this problem is hardly differentiable linearly, although you cannot say with absolute firmness.

The next option is a multilayer Neural Network option is typically used normally and has a great documentation of their practical uses, which makes it ideal for this project. This type of network is able to solve nonlinear problems, in turn, have no difficulty in dealing with nonlinear problems, which makes it an outstanding tool in the field of pattern recognition.

Finally you can emphasize that more than on par with a good design of the Neural Network is a good algorithm to train her in the previous chapter a comprehensive explanation of the operation of the algorithm backpropagation occurred while efficiency is well documented and it is supported by several libraries, making it a solid choice for system development.

5.3. ARCHITECTURE

When developing a new security system should take into account that environments that could be used, on the one hand, a scenario in which a family want to be alerted if there is a possibility of a person trespassing on their property or a scenario in which multiple cameras should be checked as in the case of large companies, closed sets or public buildings.

For these reasons the decision to solve the same problem for two different architectures take; a desktop application that is a viable option for small businesses and home environments where simple and easy thing to set up and an application on a client-server more useful platform is preferable to analyze a lot of information from different cameras are already You are in the same sector or in geographically separate areas.

Below is described as designed system that will handle solve the problem described earlier in this document. It will make use of object-oriented paradigm with which two major classes, the first charge of image analysis and the second will handle pattern recognition with Neural Network will be created to implement the prototype.

5.3.1. Image Capture

For this prototype imaging digital camera 32-bit, conditioned to take pictures at a size of 640 pixels by 480 pixels in RGB format is used. These photos are stored on your computer and read when the operator deems necessary to allow processing and decision-making software, plus a control image was saved with only the background image.

To avoid high complexity of the problem, these images will be taken in a controlled environment in which variables such as brightness and the presence of objects that may hinder the decision process are controlled.

In this first version of the prototype, it will work this way but the final idea is to use a digital camera that periodically take a picture of the sector is watching.

5.4. IMAGE PROCESSING

5.4.1. Conversión RGB to Grayscale

To simplify the processing of the image, this should (if in RGB format) to be converted to grayscale, so there are only 256 values to compare.

5.4.2. Background Separation

The first thing you will do is differentiate the background of the important objects in the image, for this average is computed and the variance of the intensity of each pixel using some initial images (in which no object present). It is assumed that the background is relatively stationary and the use of an adaptive threshold (x, y) for each pixel p (x, y), because there may be noise. Each pixel of the image is compared with an image pixel corresponding control to extract the test objects [6]. τ

For each pixel the object image is classified according to the following inequality:

If | p (x, y) – u (x, y) | < *(X, y)*

Then, it is a background pixel

p (x, y) = 0

(black)

If not

Then, it is a pixel of an object

p (x, y) = 255 (white)

Finally, a binary image which can distinguish the background and the objects to be analyzed is obtained.

5.4.3. Morphological Operations

In order to extract the silhouette image, this noise is removed using morphological operations as dilation and erosion [6]. First of all an erosion which is intended to remove noise that has been produced by the above process, then a dilation avoids takes the object to be analyzed is disconnected from one of its parts, and then another erosion so that the object has the same proportions as the original.

5.4.4. Removing the border

For extraction algorithm is applied using a Sobel variation shown in [12]. In this variation, instead of only using two convolution masks for horizontal and vertical, four masks are used; one for horizontal and one for vertical, one for the right diagonal and left diagonal to another. Partial equations can be written as:

$$S_V = (a_2 + ca_3 + a_4) - (a_0 + ca_7 + a_6)$$

$$S_H = (a_0 + ca_1 + a_2) - (a_4 + ca_5 + a_6)$$

$$S_{DI} = (a_1 + ca_2 + a_3) - (a_7 + ca_6 + a_5)$$

$$S_{DD} = (a_1 + ca_0 + a_7) - (a_3 + ca_4 + a_5)$$

With c = 2;

The above equations can be expressed with the following convolution masks.

$$S_H = \begin{matrix} 1 & 2 & 1 \\ 0 & 0 & 0 \\ -1 & -2 & -1 \end{matrix} \qquad S_V = \begin{matrix} -1 & 0 & 1 \\ -2 & 0 & 2 \\ -1 & 0 & 1 \end{matrix}$$

$$S_{DI} = \begin{matrix} 0 & 1 & 2 \\ -1 & 0 & 1 \\ -2 & -1 & 0 \end{matrix}$$

$$S_{DD} = \begin{matrix} 2 & 1 & 0 \\ 1 & 0 & -1 \\ 0 & -1 & -2 \end{matrix}$$

These four measures are known for the magnitude and phase of the gradient. The magnitude of the gradient can be estimated as [12].

$$Magnitude = Max[|S_H|, |S_V|, |S_{GAVE}|, |S_{DD}|] + 1/8\,[|S|]$$

$\perp$

where $S\perp$ It is the extent perpendicular to the maximum direction. The magnitude is compared with a threshold to determine if a pixel edge, if the pixel is detected is represented with a 255 (white), otherwise, it is represented by 0 (black).

5.4.5. Feature Extraction

5.4.5.1. Representation of the Border

The technique used is to represent the edge as a string of codes. Assuming that each pixel is connected to its eight neighbors (8-connectivity), each time a neighboring pixel is in the chain a number representing the address of that pixel [6] is entered. The contour is retracted from any point in the direction of clockwise to generate chain codes contour image.

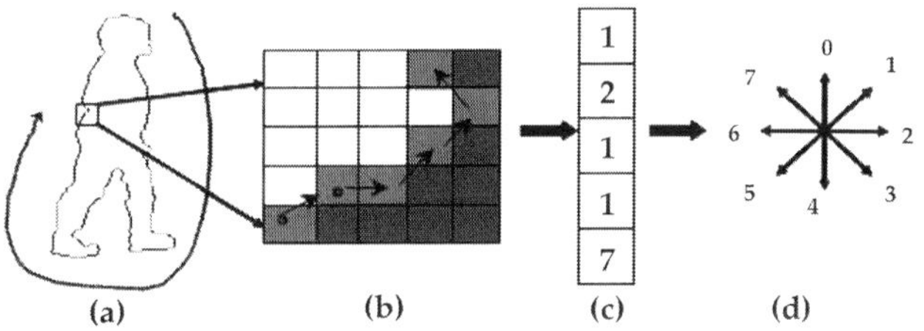

Figure 5.2. Representation human silhouette contour, (*Source: self-made or CC-BY license*).

Classification requires that the relevant features are extracted from the code string representing the contour of the silhouette [6]. The frequency $f_j(K)$ a value $v_j(K)$ is the number of tuples in the ratio R with the attribute $X_j = v_j(K)$. The representation of the silhouette can be approximated as a data distribution D_j. In the case where the silhouette is represented by a string of codes, the distribution D_j. It can be evaluated as the histogram of a codestring generated [6] for each image. Data distribution is constructed from addressability attribute.

To ensure that there is no variance based on the closeness or distance of the object to be analyzed is necessary to normalize the vector directions so that the average is zero, thus all values of this vector are among:

$$\left[-\frac{1}{k},1-\frac{1}{k}\right]$$

If f (i) is the frequency of the i-th tuple of data distribution, the i-th component of the vector, the normalized frequency can be written as:

$$\phi_i = \frac{f(i)}{\sum_{i=1}^{k} f} - \frac{1}{k}$$

But to facilitate the work it will be used with a simplified formula:

$$\phi_i = \frac{f(i)}{\sum_{i=1}^{k} f} \, para$$

Finally, the vector is constructed based on the border will be used as input to the Neural Network.

5.4.6. Neuronal Network

5.4.6.1. Design

To solve the problem a multilayer Neural Network will be used for each position to be detected (walking, front, etc.). The design is the same but for each position is trained individually, the input layer is composed of 8 neurons receiving information distribution normalized data then is input to the neurons of the hidden layer and the end layer output has only one neuron that is responsible for reporting whether the analyzed image corresponds to the position that the Neural Network must detect.

This approach to the problem allows to avoid the creation of a complex Neural Network that could cause problems like not being able to easily accommodate your parameters and require a large amount of data to be trained and instead make use of a group of simpler Neural Networks simply they train differently for each only identify a single figure.

5.4.6.2. Training

Within the database are two types of data, one for training and the other for testing. The data for training are composed of those corresponding to the various positions to be detected by the data of different objects that may be present in an enclosed space and finally valid data but does not refer to any object or to any position.

The minimum amount of data for training is given by the statement "If the network has n inputs, h hidden units, and outputà *the number of training vectors must be greater than* $n * h + h = (n + 1) * h$ *variable weights*" [14].

If the network does not converge to a solution will be tested with different numbers of neurons in the hidden layer to achieve that can perform the work in an acceptable manner.

5.4.7. Interface

As one of the parts of the project implementation, the interface design is of great importance because it represents the way in which the user interacts with the application. As mentioned in the previous chapter this project will be developed taking into account two different architectures, then the way in which the user to communicate with each will be explained.

5.4.7.1. Desktop

Usually, interfaces for desktop applications are designed to allow the user to easily work with a visual environment. This project is no exception, as stated above, this is a prototype so the interface is not very polished, but enough to allow a user with little instruction can handle it.

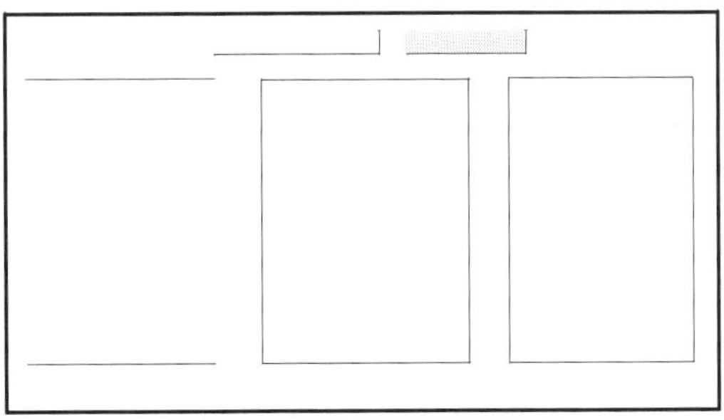

Figure 5.4. Interface design for desktop application, (*Source: self-made or CC-BY license*).

As shown in Figure 4.2 is a simple design, on top of the application space where the user will enter the name of the image to be scanned, below this space 3 images are displayed, representing will encounter the various stages image analysis. Then depending on the response of the Neural Network, an alarm will be both visual and audible warning to give the user who is using it was launched.

5.4.7.2. Client-Server

For this architecture design is different than would be used in the desktop application; as is usual in such architectures, it is sometimes necessary to sacrifice visual appeal to focus using the processor to the problem analysis. For this reason, it was decided that the operation of the application is console, limiting visual development of it.

Both the client and the server will force the user to have a better understanding of the application and work with minimal visual aid, on the client side spaces where you must type the name of the image to use and response provides will show the server. The server will display a reduced amount of information about what the system is processing as it sent the client and the response it produces. For the customer how to give an alarm will sound mainly.

To implement the system was made using a laptop compaq v2250 with Turion 64 1.8 GHz processor and 1Gb RAM with Ubuntu 8.04 operating system. To make the system to be easily migrated to other operating systems programming language C ++ with GNU GCC 4.2 compiler used. Image analysis for a free library called CImg and working with other Neural Networks known as FANN free library is used.

- **CImg** (C ++ Template Image processing tool) is a library for image processing which has as its main features being simple to use, portable between different operating systems.
- **FANN** (Fast Artificial Neural Network) is a C library for handling Neural Networks, allows the use of all or part connected multilayer networks.

These libraries were selected over others doing similar work mainly because they have a lot of documentation that facilitates the learning task, in addition, both libraries are easy to use and have no proprietary licenses that can be used at no cost by anyone wanting use them.

Since the implementation of the prototype was said in the previous chapter was developed in an object-oriented C ++ language paradigm, the prototype is based on two classes, the first charge of image analysis and the second Neural Network. This design allows it easy to use the same project for different approaches. The first approach is oriented to an application running on a computer and the second for a client-server architecture.

Being a prototype, the photos are previously taken in a controlled environment with a digital camera setting with a white background, objects dark color and lighting that prevents the formation of shadows, as these hinder the extraction of image features. The application analyzes these images and entered into the database to analyze the characteristics of the image, what position they belong and if the image will be used for training the Neural Network or for testing.

5.5. TRAINING PROCESS

Before starting work with the prototype, it was necessary to train the Neural Network so that it operates in accordance with the needs of the problem. For training, the Neural Network was first necessary to take pictures and enter the database features with which it is to identify a position of the human figure. The system has a simple module which works in console for this purpose. The experimental data of the two positions that are considered to be detected by the prototype and some objects without resembling a human silhouette.

Table 5.1. Code String Human Silhouettes Walking

Position No. 1 (Walking)

	F1	F2	F3	F4	F5	F6	F7	F8
11.jpg	0.057656	0.300567	0.0727788	0.0482042	0.0604915	0.335539	0.0359168	0.0888469
35.jpg	0.0577617	0.283394	0.0812274	0.0478339	0.0749097	0.307762	0.0406137	0.106498
54.jpg	0.0413369	0.299912	0.0879508	0.0474934	0.0466139	0.335092	0.0483729	0.0932278

Table 5.2. Code String Stops Against Human Silhouettes

Position No. 2 (Front Standing)

	F1	F2	F3	F4	F5	F6	F7	F7
90.jpg	0.0351035	0.369937	0.0675068	0.0207021	0.0423042	0.369937	0.060306	0.0342034
103.jpg	0.0402299	0.326765	0.0648604	0.0517241	0.0484401	0.342365	0.0418719	0.0837438
106.jpg	0.0478943	0.345995	0.0528489	0.0396367	0.0561519	0.355904	0.0355078	0.0660611

Table 5.3. Chain Code no Objects Like Human Silhouettes

Various objects

	F1	F2	F3	F4	F5	F6	F7	F7
131.jpg	0.00341297	0.00341297	0.0477816	0.221843	0.204778	0.450512	0.0443686	0.0238908
167.jpg	0.0241228	0.111842	0.166667	0.192982	0.0197368	0.127193	0.157895	0.199561
162.jpg	0.0798226	0.125277	0.0388027	0.252772	0.0587583	0.172949	0.0133038	0.258315

As explained in previous chapters, the vector enters the Neural Network is composed of the frequency with which each of the eight directions you can take a pixel to join another when crossing the border appears in the code string.

In reviewing the experimental data in Tables 5.1 and 5.2 may see a similarity between the data that make up each of the tables which undoubtedly indicates the presence of a pattern, but it is also visible that between tables values have their differences.

When looking at Table 5.3 is a clear difference with certain objects with a human silhouette based on the frequency of addresses, which can be inferred is that although the data in Tables 5.1 and 5.2 are not completely similar, if they are in the light of other objects that have analyzed. For this reason and the lack of data to train the Neural Network decided to work with a single Neural Network which is responsible for determining whether a high or low probability of a human figure is found either forward position or walking.

In the end, after training a configuration file that stores information network it was created, so it can be transported to different computers without the need to be reprogrammed.

5.5.1. Experimental Results

After completion of training is tested the system with different images, some simple objects or drawings and others in which is present a human figure. These images are in .jpg format with a resolution of 480 x 640 pixels. Depending on the high or low degree of probability of finding a human form, an alarm is released and the image is saved for verification indicating the name of the photo the degree of probability.

In this first prototype system does not act autonomously taking photos that will be delivered by a camera, however, the images are ready and simply open when you want to test.

Figure 5.1 alarms following an image with a high probability of belonging to a human figure is shown, this alarm is accompanied by an alarm sound to capture the user's attention. An image is also stored with the prefix (Pr_Alta_) to be verified by an operator then. Figure 5.2 alarms for displaying an image with a low degree of probability of belonging to a human figure this is not accompanied by a sound but if an image is saved with the prefix (Pr_Baja_) for later verification.

In Figure 5.3 the set of images showing the system of an image containing a human figure shown, the first image is a grayscale, the second is the differentiation between the background and the figure. Finally, there is the image of the contour from where the information is entered into the Neural Network.

Figure 5.3. With human silhouette, (*Source: self-made or CC-BY license*).

Figure 5.4. Image without human silhouette, (*Source: self-made or CC-BY license*).

The system has proven that all human figures generate a response from the Neural Network above 0.97 below are the others, but it is possible that a certain collection of objects can generate a false alarm, as those who have resemblance to a silhouette human or simply because the path along the contour of the image and create the vector address this was similar to a human silhouette.

Table 5.4 is a table with the response of the Neural Network 15 images. 5 pictures of people walking position, these data are shown in the first 2 columns; 5 compared with feet, these data are shown in column 3 and 4; and other objects not related to a human figure.

Table 5.4. Responses to Different Images

First name		First name		First name	
images	Result	images	Result	images	Result
2.jpg	1	80.jpg	1	129.jpg	0.933336
10.jpg	0.987883	88.jpg	1	137.jpg	0.881704
12.jpg	1	92.jpg	1	138.jpg	0.86979
18.jpg	1	100.jpg	1	140.jpg	0.886426
23.jpg	0.988212	112.jpg	1	150.jpg	0.927546

As shown with this information you can determine the value of the point at which clearly human silhouettes of other objects differ. But this information also lets you change the value of that point to increase the likelihood of detecting more human forms but in this way also increases the number of false alarms.

5.5.2. Client-Server Communication

Previously the reasons why it was decided to develop the system for two different architectures were explained, the client-server application allows a central server responsible only for managing the Neural Network and a large number of customers who are responsible for image analysis. But it was necessary to decide how the client would communicate with the server and vice versa.

Thanks to previous experience it was decided that communication between the two applications was best to use messages in XML format, which are easy to construct and which is easy to retrieve information. Par implementation of this part of a library that is easy to use and has a great documentation, as well as being released under a non-exclusive license was used.

An example of the type of message being sent is displayed from the client to the server, it contains the information of the 8 inputs of the Neural Network.

<? Xml version = “1.0”?>

<Rna>

<F1> 0.90000 </ f1>

<F2> 0.91000 </ f2>

<F3> 0.92000 </ f3>

<F4> 0.93000 </ f4>

<F5> 0.94000 </ f5>
<F6> 0.95000 </ f6>
<F7> 0.96000 </ f7>
<F8> 0.97000 </ f8>
</ Rna>

The following example is a returned by the server to one of its clients message contains the response of the Neural Network and a field that in the future may be used to identify what type of individual position belongs

nervous system is a neuron; the neuron is a specialized receive and transmit electrical impulses called action potentials cell, these shock traveling dare cell membrane and is the primary means of communication between tissues and cells within the body [2]. Communication between neurons is accomplished through cellular extensions called dendrites, cell attachment between dendrites is known as synapses [4]. There is a type of specialized neurons that make up the human motor system, these neurons are called motor neurons; motoneurons are responsible for sending and receiving electrical impulses from the spine to muscle fibers [2]. The musculoskeletal system consists mainly of motor neurons, muscle fibers, muscle, and skeleton, together provide support for the body and the ability to perform movements [4]. In muscle we can distinguish between 2 units mainly anatomical and functional unit; the first is called muscle fiber, while the second is called a motor unit. The motor unit (UM) [18] is a group of muscle fibers innervated by a single motor neuron. Perform a simple movement it requires the involvement of many both sensory neurons and motor, working together to achieve perform the indicated action; the operation is as follows: the order is generated in the brain in the form of an electrical pulse; This pulse travels through the spine and reaches motoneurons innervate the muscle responsible to perform the action stimulating the muscle fibers, thereby causing expansion or inhibition of muscle. It is noteworthy that for a complex movement, say the extension or bending the arm involves many motoneurons, and cannot be achieved only by stimulating a muscle, which is linked to more than one UM (Figure 6.1).

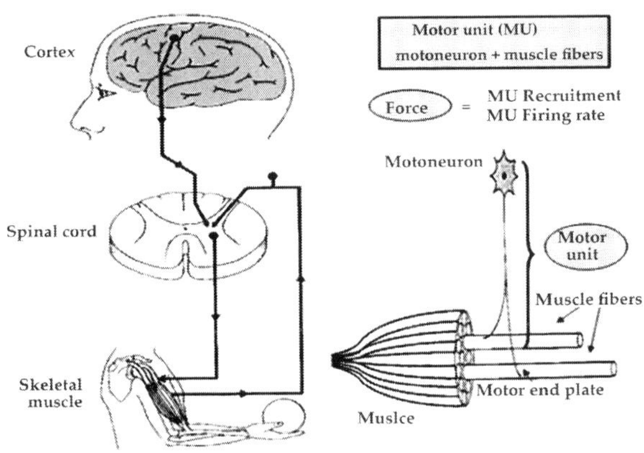

Figure 6.1. Biological process of the complex movement (*Source: self-made or CC-BY license*).

6.1. ELECTRODES

The way to get information about our environment and transfer it to an electronic apparatus is carried out by a transducer, a transducer is a device capable of transforming an input power type to another type of output power. In the field of bioelectricity transducers used they are called electrodes; the electrodes make an ionic transfer of living tissue of the body to an electronic device, which is responsible for processing it to obtain useful information later measurement [20]; among the most studied and recorded in biological signals include electrocardiographic (ECG), electroencephalogram (EEG), electromyography (EMG), to name a few (Table 6.1). For the records of these signals they are usually mainly use two types of electrodes, the surface electrodes, and invasive electrodes; the surface electrodes are placed on the skin surface and are able to take population registers of bioelectrical [17] activity; while invasive electrodes are inserted directly into the tissue to make the potential difference between the cell membrane and skin [17].

Table 6.1. Common abbreviations and sources

Bioelectric Signal	Abbreviation	Biologic Source
Electrocardiogram	ECG	Heart - as seen from body surface
Cardiac electrogram	—	Heart - as seen from within
Electromyogram	EMG	Muscle
Electroencephalogram	EEG	Brain
Electrooptigram	EOG	Eye dipole field
Electroretinogram	ERG	Eye retina
Action potential	—	Nerve or muscle
Electrogastrogram	EGG	Stomach
Galvanic skin reflex	GSR	Skin

6.2. ELECTROMYOGRAPHY

One of the main techniques to acquire information from the body is electromyography. Electromyography (EMG) is the study of electrical potentials generated by musculus during movement. H. Piper was the first researcher to study EMG in 1912 Germany, built a prototype based on a galvanometer; Gasser and Erlanger in 1924 did a similar study, but now using an oscilloscope; four years after Proebster observed signals produced by the denervation of muscles, opening the field of clinical EMG [18]. Since

1980 with the introduction of computers will be able to perform large studies and decomposition of EMG signals in a few seconds, one of the pioneers in this were LeFever and De Luca. [18].

As the electromyography aims the study of muscle activity, you cannot ignore the activity of motor units [2]; in a voluntary muscle contraction force it is modulated by a series of changes in the frequency of the activity of UMs, i.e., the firing frequency of the potentials of the UMs depends on the applied force and speed of muscle contraction. The frequency spectrum of motor units during a voluntary muscle contraction or (MVC) is shown in Figure 6.2 while Figure 6.3 shows the relationship between the voluntary muscle contraction and surface electromyographic signal [8] shown. Based on these figures, it can be seen that the most electromyographic activity is present around 50Hz [18]. In a skeletal muscle contraction, potential ranges ranging from 50μV to the 5mV [17]. There are two main ways to record the electromyographic signals; surface electromyography or non-invasive and invasive electromyography.

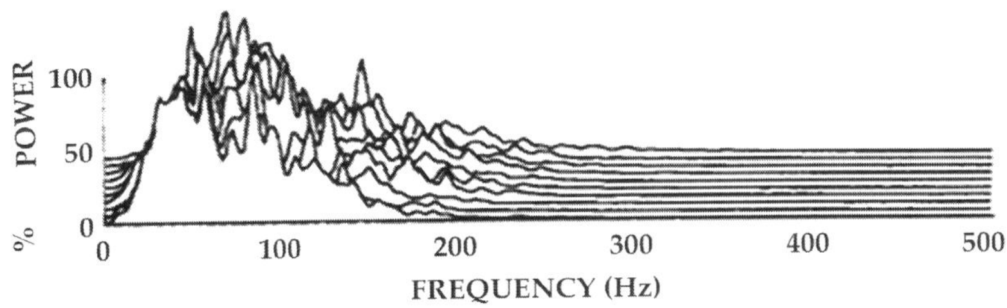

Figure 6.2. The frequency spectrum of motor units during a voluntary muscle contraction (*Source: self-made or CC-BY license*)

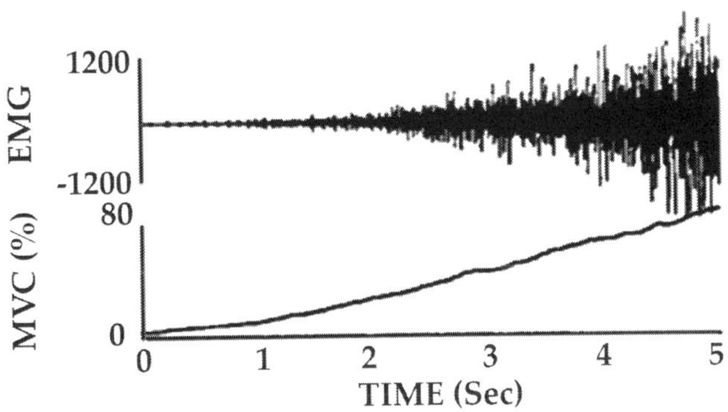

Figure 6.3. The relationship between the voluntary muscle contraction and surface electromyographic signal (*Source: self-made or CC-BY license*).

Among electromyography are two main techniques for the acquisition of the potentials generated by the motor units, these techniques are invasive electromyography and surface electromyography [17]. The muscles of the body are made up of several neurons motorcycle, which innervate specifies an area of the muscle fibers; invasive electromyography is responsible for obtaining the registration of the potential generated by a motor unit in particular. It is very useful for various fields, especially in rehabilitation, internal medicine or orthopedic surgery, used to locate the injured area, specifying whether it is a problem of a hand, arm or leg, or if more diffuse, and defining technique if the injury is a muscle, nerve, nerve root or trunk, or more than one [18].

6.2.1. Needle Electrodes

To measure the potential generated by the motor units, invasive electromyography uses needle electrodes; a needle electrode consists of a thin metal needle which is inserted directly into the muscle. Figure 6.4 shows different types of needle electrodes [18].

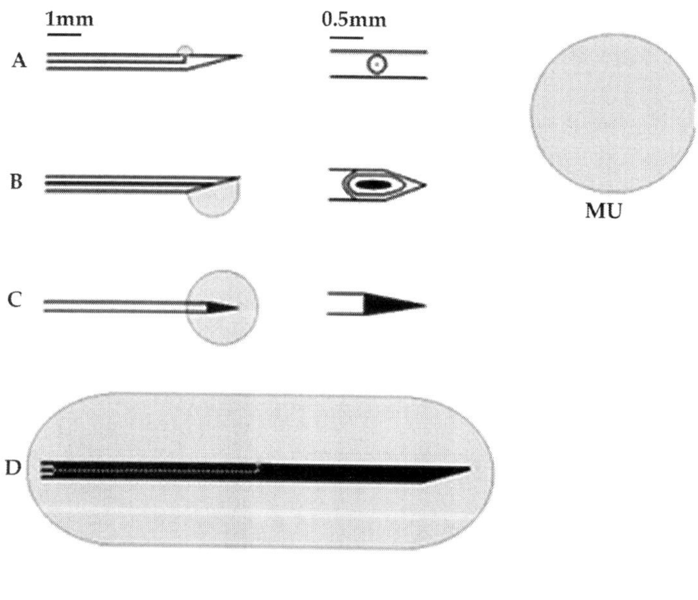

Figure 6.4. Different types of needle electrodes (*Source: self-made or CC-BY license*).

The signal amplitude recorded by the needle electrodes depends on the recording area occupied, as well as the distance to the source electrode of the (UM) signal; It is the largest amplitude when the electrode is closer to the motor unit; the amplitude decreases as far this the source electrode [18].

Because the insertion of needle electrodes is quite painful and it requires medical supervision, electromyography invasive limited to clinical and medical nature uses, is mainly used to diagnose motor diseases, this feature makes it difficult to use in research to the development of prostheses since many people find very annoying the insertion procedure.

6.2.2. Surface Electromyography

Surface electromyography or SEMG [18] is a technique that is based on the use of surface electrodes; these electrodes are placed directly on the skin muscle which you want information. The sEMG is peculiar in that the values obtained by it show population activity of motor units, this is because the electrodes, being on the surface of the muscle, are not able to capture the signal of a single motor unit, but instead, they capture information from several UMs [17]. It is for this reason that this technique is not widely used for very precise medical diagnosis. Furthermore the use of the surface electrodes is much more suitable for the study of the average behavior of the electrical activity of a muscle or muscle group, which it is widely used to detect muscle fatigue and performance monitoring of athletes; sEMG is the technique which is used primarily for the development of myoelectric prostheses, where the use of needle electrodes would not be very comfortable for the patient. Thanks to contributions from De Luca [18], the field of decomposition and detection of surface EMG signals opened, as pioneered in suggesting the study of electromyography in unit action potentials (Figure 6.5).

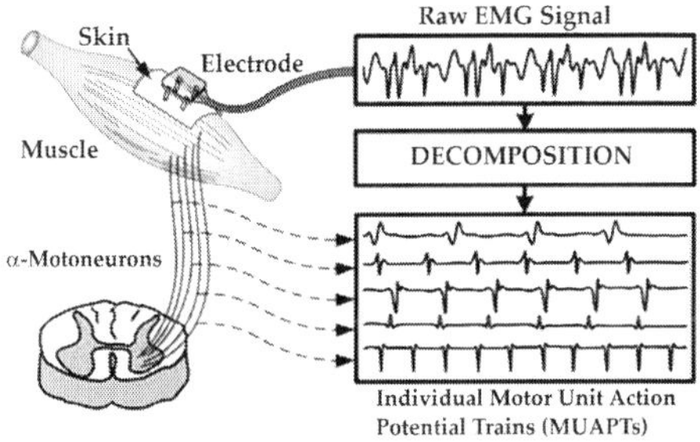

Figure 6.5. Electromyography in unit action potentials (*Source: self-made or CC-BY license*).

6.2.2.1. Surface Electrodes

The surface electrodes are placed on the skin, these electrodes are mainly metal surfaces, however, due to being in direct contact with the skin must take certain considerations [18]: the skin is a conductive fabric whose intracellular and extracellular material is compound electrolyte solutions, in which the current is carried by ions; while the metal is a highly conductive material, in which the current is carried by electrons, thus the skin-electrode interface is itself very noisy [18].

Several types of surface electrodes, these mainmind are divided into two groups: dry and wet electrodes [21]. Wet electrodes are those in which between the metal plate and the skin is an electrolytic substance or conductive gel [17], this is done in order to minimize the inherent noise generated between the skin contact and metal, this conductive gel improves conductivity and current flow (Figure 6.6).

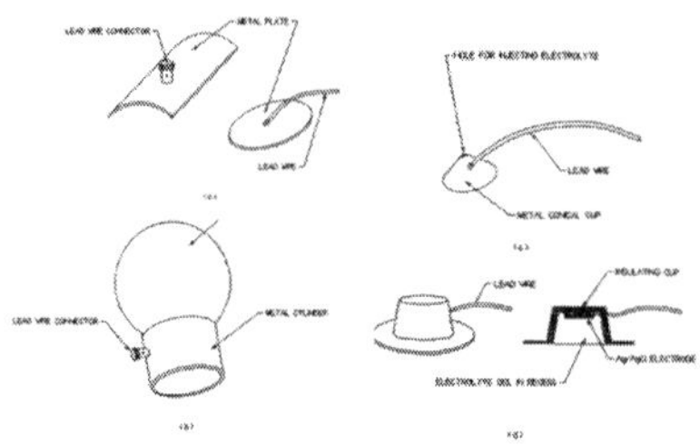

Figure 6.6. Improving the conductivity and current flow (*Source: self-made or CC-BY license*).

The materials that constitute the majority of the surface electrodes are highly variable among them are silver, gold, stainless steel, platinum, and others. As for the dry electrodes, Searle and Kirkup [21] they conducted a comparison between constructed work dry electrodes, on the background the works of several authors who had developed dry electrodes (Table 6.2). The experiment consisted in assembling three arrays of dry electrodes of different metals (aluminum, stainless steel, and titanium) and were compared against wet Ag/AgCl Figure 6.7 [21]. Measurements were made on the contact impedance; the results are shown in Figure 6.8 [21], the graphs show the impedance with respect to time; it is important to mention that you want the contact impedance between the electrode and the skin remains constant over time or as constant as possible; in experiments shows that the electrolyte interface Ag/AgCl is fairly constant, however, the purpose of this experiment was to make a comparison between the Ag/AgCl and dry electrodes highly conductive metals, finding that the electrodes titanium and stainless steel have a contact impedance response quite similar and very acceptable when compared with the Ag/AgCl.

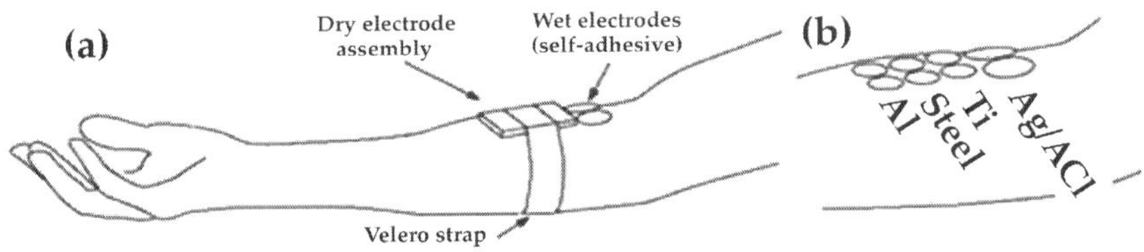

Figure 6.7 Assembling three arrays of dry electrodes of different metals (aluminum, stainless steel, and titanium) (*Source: self-made or CC-BY license*).

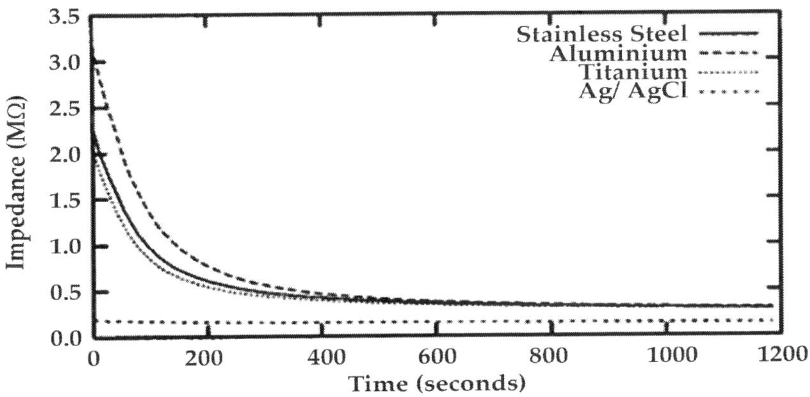

Figure 6.8. Results of the measurements(*Source: self-made or CC-BY license*).

One of the desirable conditions in an electrode is polarized than it means that the potential at the electrode should not vary considerably increasing the current to pass through it; the silver electrode silver (Ag/AgCl) chloride has shown adequate standards to achieve this feature; Additional skin-skin interface or silver-Ag/AgCl has the highest resistive impedance in the frequency domain in EMG [21].

6.2.3. Location of the Electrodes, Shape, Size, Distance and Inter-Electrode Material

One of the most discussed points in the surface EMG is the location of the electrodes. Because of this, a European initiative to try to standardize these factors originated; location, size, and shape of the electrodes; Thus the SENIAM (Surface Electromyography for Noninvasive Assessment of Muscles) arises in 1996 to try to make certain recommendations for these variables [5]. In many references, where its theme is the SEMG were several records of different configurations in the size and position of the electrodes. Figure 6.9a shows the values of the diameter of the electrodes taken by several publications and European works, it can be seen that the preferred steps to electrode diameter are 10 mm [18]. The inter-electrode distance is defined as the center to center distance of the conductive electrode area [18]. Figure 6.9b shows information collected references the inter-electrode distance used in them. The electrode shape is defined as the conductive area that contacts the skin. Most references match the circular shape as the most used [18].

The material used for the electrodes is silver-silver chloride (Ag/AgCl) combination; these electrodes are usually manufactured by electrolysis. Silver two discs are made and are immersed in a saline solution. The positive pole of a DC source is connected to the disc to be chlorinated silver and the negative pole is connected to the other disk. A stream to a cup of 1 mA/cm^2 is passed through the electrode for a few minutes. A layer of silver chloride is then deposited on the anode surface [18].

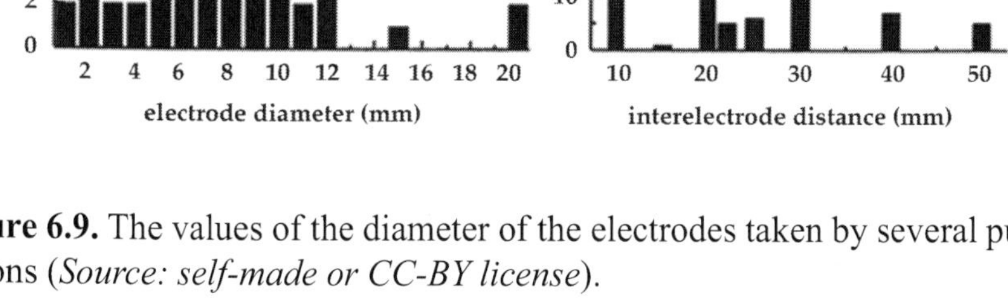

Figure 6.9. The values of the diameter of the electrodes taken by several publications (*Source: self-made or CC-BY license*).

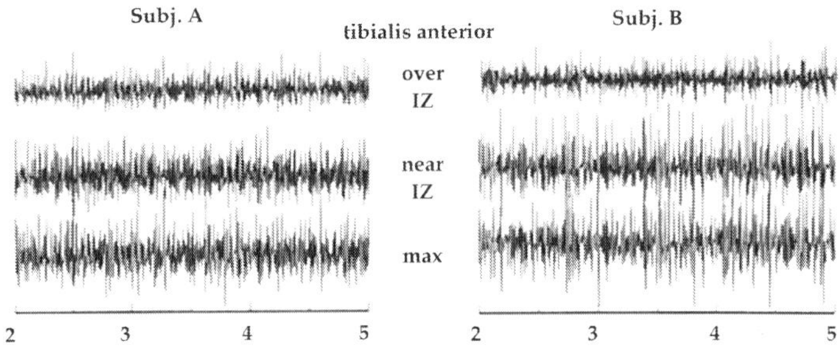

Figure 6.10. Variations in signal amplitude SEMG in different positions (*Source: self-made or CC-BY license*).

The SENIAM [5] provides a series of steps performed before measurements SEMG: (1) selection of electrodes for SEMG. (2) Preparation of the skin, this implies either amplification of a conductive gel or cleaning with alcohol the area where the electrodes are to be placed. (3) Positioning the patient in the initial position, this position can vary depending on the study to be performed. (4) Determine the location of the electrodes. (5) Fix the electrodes. (6) Finally testing the connections. These measures for trying to standard methods, materials, positions and size of the electrodes, are well deserved, as measurement of sEMG is quite variable and it is very difficult to replicate experiments and obtaining the [same values [5]; one of the factors involved is that the amplitude of the sEMG signal increases relative to the longitudinal displacement of the electrode on the muscle. Figure 6.10 shows variations in signal amplitude SEMG in different positions.

6.3. ELECTRONIC FUNDAMENTALS

For the construction of a electromyograph, which is a device for acquiring signals from the muscles, is necessary to consider several factors, among them, are the pre-signal amplification, signal filtering, and analog-digital. Before talking about the stages of electromyography, it is convenient to define some concepts of electronics.

6.3.1. Operational Amplifier

The operational amplifier is an integrated circuit composed of a large number of transistors [1]. This circuit is very popular because of its versatility, may be used in multiple settings and are capable of arithmetic operations such as addition, subtraction, integration, and differentiation. The diagram of an amplifier is presented in Figure 6.11; the terminal which has appreciated; the Vout terminal is the output terminal, the V- terminal is the non-inverting input, the V + terminal is the non-inverting input, while the Vs + and Vs- terminals are the supply terminals, the Vs- is negative and the Vs + it is the positive supply. Operational [1] has the characteristic amplifiers amplify the potential difference appearing at its terminals V_+ and V_- giving a gain A, ideally infinite; Vout = A ($V_+ - V_-$).

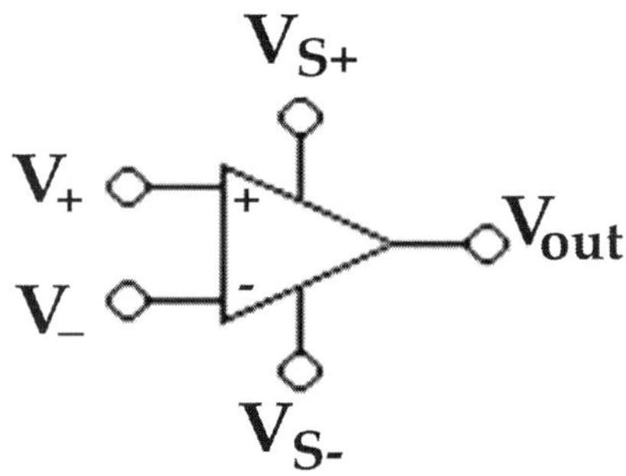

Figure 6.11. The diagram of an amplifier (*Source: self-made or CC-BY license*).

The model of ideal operational amplifier circuit is considered that it has the following characteristics [1]: infinite input impedance, that is, that the net current flowing into the amplifier non-inverting and inverting terminals is zero; zero output impedance; zero common-mode gain, this translates to the fact that by applying equal voltages to the inputs, the amplifier output should be zero [1]; A gain infinite open, in other words, loop can amplify the factor (V + – V–) to infinite values; and the bandwidth is infinite, this is the ideal operational amplifiers can amplify signals in the frequency ranges from 0 to infinity with infinite [3] gain. However, these features cannot be achieved at all in reality, a very simple example is the fact that we cannot give infinite profits, since the actual operational amplifier can only give gain depending on the range of its power supplies, give an infinite gain equivalent to having infinite sources of supply, which is not possible in practice; while on the side of infinite input impedance, it is not possible, but the market there are amplifiers having input impedances of several hundred mega ohms, which can make approaches to the model of the ideal operational amplifier.

Amplifiers operations have various types of configurations, including the most commonly used are:

6.3.1.1. The Inverting Configuration

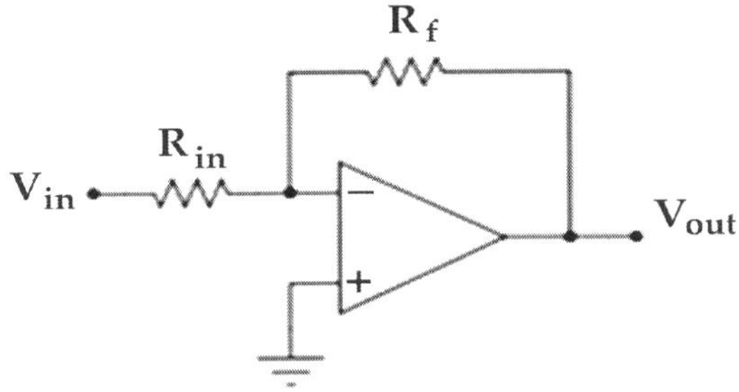

Figure 6.12. The analogue diagram (*Source: self-made or CC-BY license*).

Named due to the operation performed, the diagram is shown in Figure 6.12 [1]; this configuration outputs the amplified value of input voltage Vin based on the following formula [1]:

$$Vout = -\frac{R2}{R1} Vin.$$

6.3.1.2. Non-Inverting Configuration

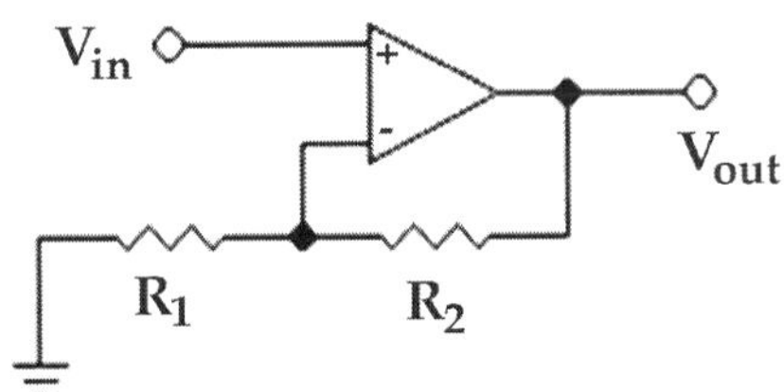

Figure 6.13. The analogue diagram (*Source: self-made or CC-BY license*).

This configuration is shown in Figure 6.13. Called because the output Vout resulting amplified value of input voltage (Vin) based on the following formula [1]:

$$Vout = \left(\frac{R2}{R1} + 1\right) Vin.$$

6.3.1.3. The Voltage Follower

The voltage follower configuration is simple enough, the value of the output voltage is equal to the input voltage, it is said that the output follows the input. Its configuration is shown in Figure 6.14 [1].

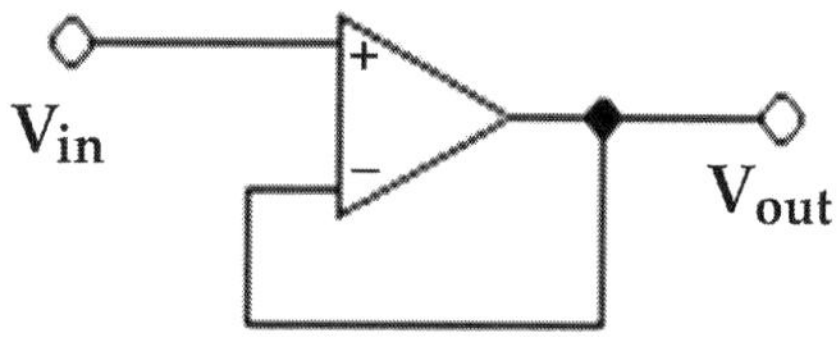

Figure 6.14. The analogue diagram (*Source: self-made or CC-BY license*).

6.3.1.4. Differential Amplifier

A differential amplifier is one that amplifies the potential difference at its inputs (Figure 6.15).

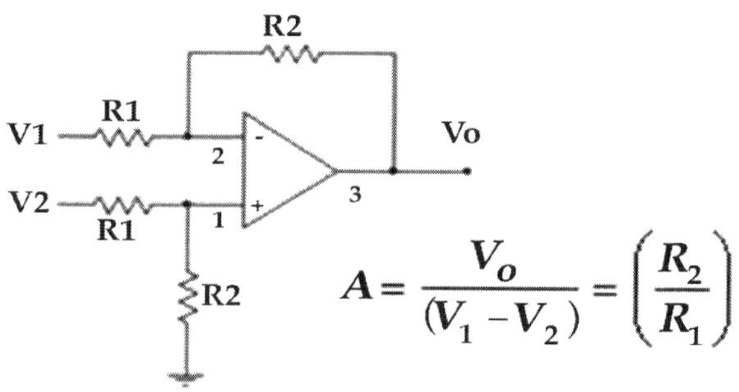

Figure 6.15. The analogue diagram (*Source: self-made or CC-BY license*).

6.3.1.5. Half-Wave Rectifier Precision

A rectifier circuit is one that converts the negative signal components of a positive; Two types of rectification: half-wave rectification and full wave, the medium wave retains the positive signal components while the full wave becomes the negative components of the input signal to positive leaving intact positive components, different types of grinding are shown in Figure 6.16 [2].

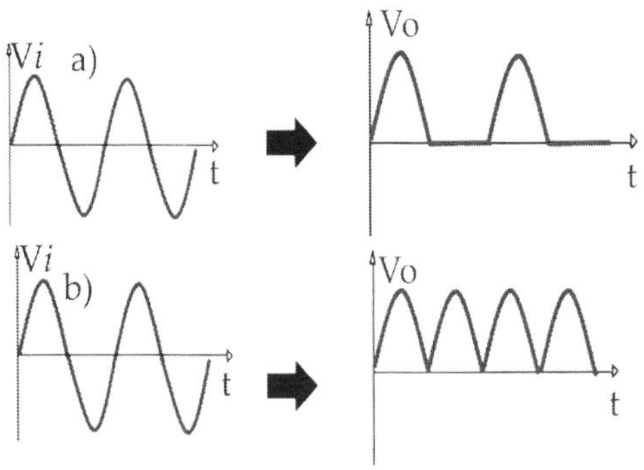

Figure 6.16. Different types of grinding (*Source: self-made or CC-BY license*).

The half wave rectifier precision or "super LED" [1], named because it behaves as a diode but no loss of 0.7 volts typical voltage diodes [1], thus is able to rectify the signal that is applied with great accuracy. Figure 6.17 shows the configuration of this circuit.

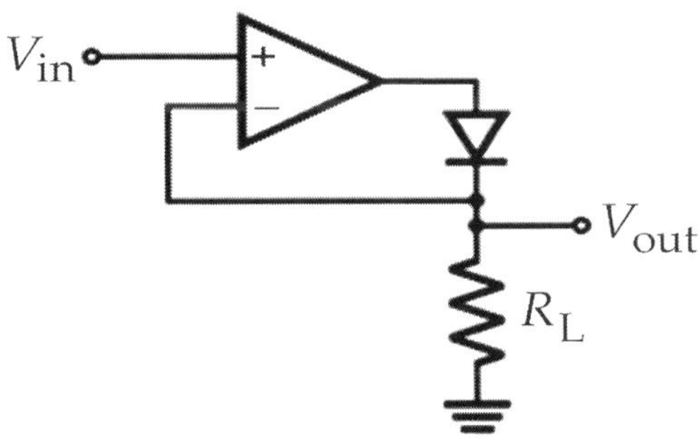

Figure 6.17. The configuration of this circuit Source: self-made or CC-BY license.

6.3.1.6. Comparator Circuit

The comparator circuits are used to detect when a signal exceeds a voltage level [1]; comparing the voltage value of an input signal (Vin) against a value of a reference voltage (Vref), its operation is very simple, the only changes dissociates saturation values –Vsat + Vsat to its output when the Vin signal on passing the limit imposed by the reference voltage Vref (comparator noninverting) (Figure 6.20). In other words, the comparator will only have two outputs:

- Vout = + Vsat when Vin> Vref
- Vout = –Vsat when Vin <Vref

6.3.1.7. Integrator Circuit

The integrating circuit is a operational amplifier configuration (Figure 6.18) [1]; This circuit has an output proportional to the area under the curve of the voltage input voltage; i.e., the integral of the input voltage but inverted in phase, this is because the configuration is the inverting amplifier configuration.

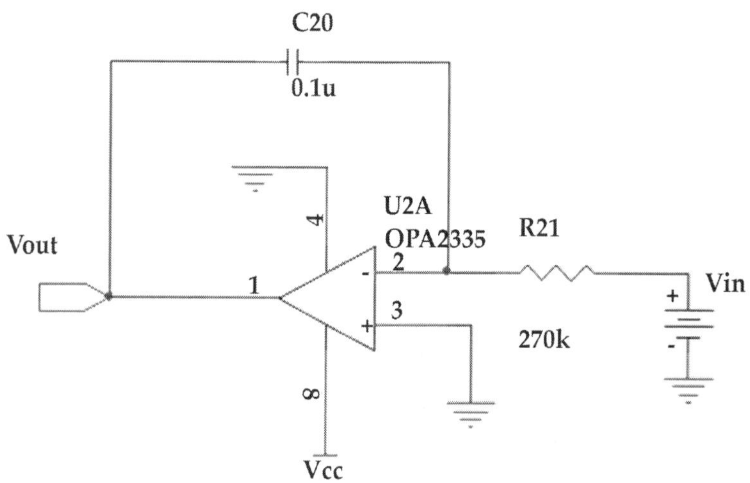

Figure 6.18. operational amplifier configuration (*Source: self-made or CC-BY license*).

6.4. THE ELECTROMYOGRAPH

The electromyograph is an electronic device used to record the electrical activity of muscles, this device usually has a screen where you can visualize action potentials of motor units, also it has several sets of electrodes and a small interface control measurements [17]. To register EMG needle electrodes, which are inserted directly into muscle often used; it is also possible to use surface electrodes. SEMG measurements for three surface electrodes two electrodes are required to capture the potential difference in muscle and a ground electrode, which serves as a benchmark for measurements. The electrodes pick up the action potentials of motor units action,

6.4.1. Stage Preamp

The amplitude of the EMG signals depends on several factors; position, type, and material of the electrodes used; a typical EMG signal has amplitude ranges ranging from 0.1 to 0.5 mV. This signal may contain frequency components that extend to 10kHz [17]. The preamplifier is generally used for EMG differential type and its input impedance should be 109 – 1012Ω in parallel with a capacitor 2 – 10pF; It is also advisable to place the preamplifier fairly close to the electrodes and the subject, thus capacitances and problems caused parasites by movement artifacts and cable are avoided. Another important feature is the common mode rejection or CMRR for short English (Common Mode Rejection Ratio) [1], this term is defined for the differential amplifiers as:

$$CMRR = 20log_{10}\left(\frac{Ad}{Ac}\right)$$

$$Ad = \frac{Vo}{V2 - V1}, differential\ mode$$

$$Ac = common\ mode$$

The CMRR is measured in decibels and is the ratio between the gain difference mode (V2 – V1) and the common-mode gain (ideally zero). EMG measurements for rejection of common mode 90db minimum required.

One of the arrangements with amplifiers operations more preamplifier is used as instrumentation amplifier [1]. This circuit comprises three amplifiers and serves to amplify the voltage difference present at its inputs (V1 and V2). The instrumentation amplifier has the characteristic of having high input impedances and quite high CMRR. They are often used to amplify very small signals, for example, signals of the human body (Figure 6.19).

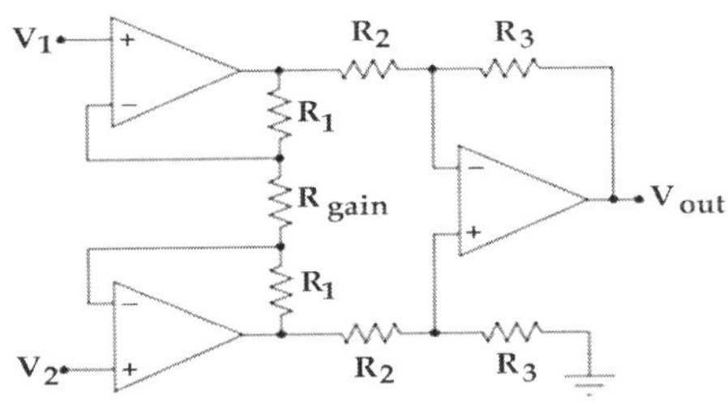

Figure 6.19. Amplifying signals of the human body (*Source: self-made or CC-BY license*).

6.4.2. Stage Filter

The step from preamp amplified signal containing a mixture of biological signals, for example, are immersed ECG signals, and depending on where breathing could find traces of EEG. It is for this reason that to have clear records of EMG is necessary to purify or filter information; this is achieved using amplifiers operations with analog filters which are constructed for only records EMG, these signals are presented in the frequency range 10 to 500 Hz [18]. However, the noise signals from the movement of the cables and artifacts are between 0 and 15, which is why it is preferred to have a filter 15 to 500 Hz or 20 to 500 Hz in many published works, depending on what desired. Another technique to avoid noise from the outlet and the atmosphere is appending a reject bands notch 50 or 60 Hz filter, however it has some complications, in the case of the EMG as many components of these potentials are about 50 and 60 Hz [17], so that if this technique noise reduction will apply valuable information would be lost. For filtering the signal, there are multiple configurations, must also take into account the order of the filter; the filter order is an important factor and helps greatly reducing noise. Figure 6.20 [18] shows a typical EMG potential which has been applied filtrates first and second order.

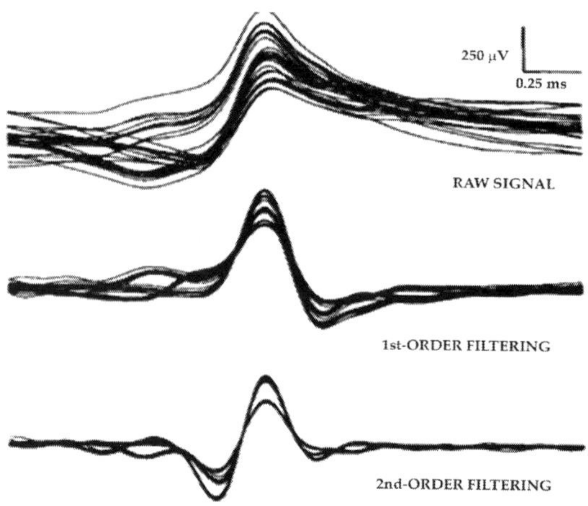

Figure 6.20. EMG potential which has been applied filtrates first and second order.

(*Source: self-made or CC-BY license*).

6.4.3. Conversion Analog Digital

Analog-digital conversion (A/D), is the process by which continuous signals or real world are transformed to voltage levels representing a binary code [17]. A continuous signal is one that can theoretically take any value in scope and not limited to a finite number of points. A/D converter accepts signals in a specific voltage range, for example, ± 5V, which is subdivided into a number of discrete levels, this number is given by the formula 2n-1, where n is the number of bits of the converter A/D. The digitization process consists of several steps: sampling, retention, quantization, and coding. Sampling is the stage where the continuous signal samples are taken; the sampling rate depends on an internal clock and called the sampling frequency. The holding step is responsible for maintaining the value of the sample for sufficient time that can be processed. The quantization process consists in measuring the voltage value received and assigning a single output value. Finally, the encoding step is to translate the quantized to a binary value. One of the main disadvantages of the conversion process A/D is the loss of information due to truncation and rounding when coding and the appearance of the effect called "aliasing"; the effect "aliasing" is to obtain a different sampled signal when trying to reconstruct the original analog signal. To avoid this effect, it is desirable to use the Nyquist sampling theorem [18]; This theorem states that a signal can be completely reconstructed without loss of information if it is sampled at a frequency of at least twice the largest harmonic present in the analog signal. In the case of muscles, the frequency for the largest surface electromyography harmonic is in the range of 400–450 Hz [18].

People who have motor problems, either muscular atrophy, amputations or absence of limb from birth cannot perform certain tasks of daily life. However, thanks to advances in medicine and electronics, the field of myoelectric prosbook was developed, these systems are responsible for registering and translate electrical impulses from muscle natural arm movements. To help people with motor problems arises the field of comfortable myoelectric prosthetics and not showing him any difficulties or inconveniences the patient This study was designed taking into account the needs of patients and versatility of the final device, since being employed,

The book focuses on the acquisition and signal processing myoelectric, specifically arm muscles to subsequently obtain a pulse LVTTL (Low Voltage Transistor-Transistor Logic) [1] Corresponding to the actions of the potential of the muscle fibers. In the future, with this output, LVTTL is to make a parallelization stage such that each motion corresponds a binary number from 10 only bits. He system current end funcna with 3.3 volts and can acquire the signals from the biceps and triceps muscles [4]; this system produces pulses of LVTTL levels according to the detected muscular excitation, for in the future such use these outputs and connect them to an artificial Neural Network to recognize movement patterns.

System development is divided into several stages before having completed the prototype. The first development was acquisition system with certain limitations. This prototype served as a reference for subsequent developments, we call this prototype "prototype EMG Acquisition Source Bipolar." The next development to which we will call "Prototype Acquisition single channel EMG LVTTL" features major improvements over the previous, both in design and efficiency, however you can only take EMG signals from a muscle; finally it developed the "Prototype Acquisition EMG two channels," which is able to take at the same time the EMG signals of two different muscles.

The acquisition system developed electromyographic signals consists of several stages. Figure 6.24 shows the block diagram of the system for the acquisition of EMG single channel.

6.5. DESIGN AND CONSTRUCTION OF THE PROTOTYPE FOR THE ACQUISITION OF ELECTROMYOGRAPHIC SIGNALS WITH BIPOLAR SOURCE

The first prototype constructed followed the steps shown in Figure 6.21, so their development comprising the steps of preamplification, filtering, final amplification, rectification and with the only exception that instead of stage A/D conversion this prototype uses a comparator circuit to convert the EMG signals to square pulses.

Because the electromyographic signal has amplitudes in the range of 500μV [17], it is necessary to cascade series of amplification. In this prototype, the chain gains shown in Figure 6.22; It is the total amplification of the system 2107; thus EMG signal of 500μV will have a value of 1,053 volts. To achieve amplifications, operational amplifiers are used in non-inverting configuration, this is done in order not to alter the phase of the output.

An important in the construction of this prototype point is the use of two power supplies (9V battery), hence the name "bipolar source"; this feature has certain disadvantages, and the most obvious is the use of the two 9V batteries (Figure 6.23), this is due to the characteristics of the integrated circuits used, as these were not manufactured to operate at lower levels of voltage 5V.

6.5.1. Electrodes

The first thing to be considered before the acquisition of EMG signals is the type of electrodes to be used; in this first prototype, the electrodes must meet certain characteristics to perform the various tests in a simple and practical way; These features are:

- The electrodes must be able to be assembled and disassembled in a clean and easy way to avoid medical supervision.
- The electrodes should be able to capture the EMG signal with an appropriate level of noise.

Taking into account these characteristics, we chose to work with disposable surface electrodes of Ag/AgCl 3M brand Figure 6.24.

This electrodes are used for ECG and are able to capture EMG signals [17]; besides medical supervision is required at the time of application to the muscle. The electrodes were placed to record muscle activity of the biceps muscle. Three electrodes for acquisition, the investor electrode, the non-inverting reference and used; the investor and non-inverting electrodes are separated by a distance of 2 cm inter-electrode while the reference electrode was placed on the wrist. Figure 6.25 shows the position of the electrodes relative to the arm.

6.5.2. Preamplification Stage

In step preamp an instrumentation amplifier was used. This, in turn, must meet certain characteristics to have good performance in acquiring biological signals, these features are mainly:

- Input impedance should be 109 – 1012Ω || 2 – 10pF.
- ≥ 90dB CMRR.
- Bias current input (input bias current) ≤ 20nA.

Taking these characteristics is, chose to use the instrumentation amplifier INA129 Texas Instruments (Figure 6.21), this amplifier has the following characteristics:

- Input bias current: 5NA max.

- CMRR: 120dB min.
- Power Supply ± 2,25V to ± 18V.
- Differential input impedance: 1010Ω || 2 pF.

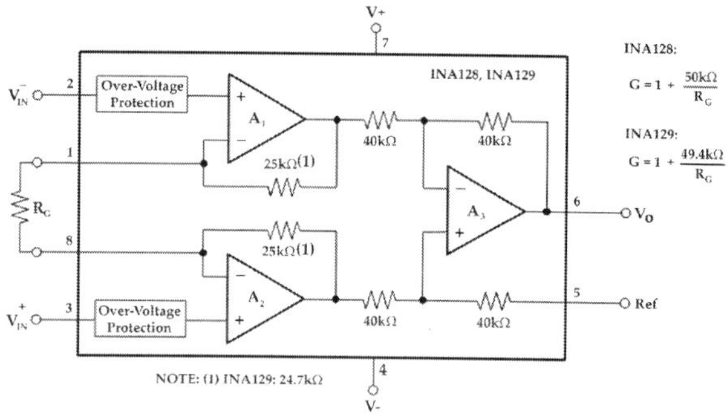

Figure 6.21. The instrumentation amplifier INA129 (*Source: self-made or CC-BY license*).

The INA129 is one instrumentation amplifiers commonly used to have very good features, such as its high CMRR (120dB), however, this amplifier is the type of bipolar source, i.e., its operation is designed to work with two sources feeding.

The gain of the preamplifier is divided into two, the gain of the instrumentation amplifier and the gain of an operational amplifier in noninverting configuration. The calculation of the strength to set the gain of INA129 shown, considering that the desired gain is 10. Using the formula provided by the manufacturer becomes [8]:

$$G_{ina129} = 1 + \frac{49.4k\Omega}{R_G}$$

$$10 = 1 + \frac{49.4k\Omega}{R_G} \rightarrow \frac{9}{49.4k\Omega} = \frac{1}{R_G} \rightarrow R_G = 5.48k\Omega \approx 5.6k\Omega$$

$$R_G = 5.6k\Omega$$

Additionally, a feedback circuit or driver with his right proposed by the manufacturer was integrated [8] used to record ECG signals or ECG (Figure 6.22). If the position of EMG electrodes RA and placing them around the muscle and RL electrode as the reference electrode which is placed on the wrist was modified. This feedback loop serves to avoid current imbalance and offset problems common mode noise differential input instrumentation amplifier.

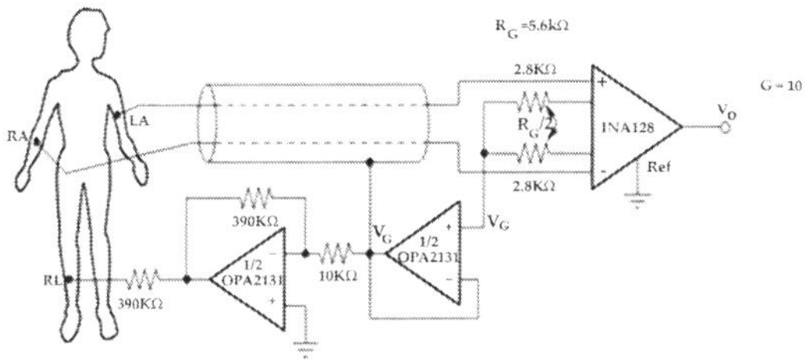

Figure 6.22. Process of recording ECG signals (*Source: self-made or CC-BY license*).

The modifications made to the circuit right leg ECG shown in the schematic diagram of Figure 6.23; Note that there is an exit labeled "Malla," this output is connected to the shielding layer that should have lead wire electrodes. The advantage of having the shield mesh is that leakage currents that may appear between the conductors of the electrodes are avoided.

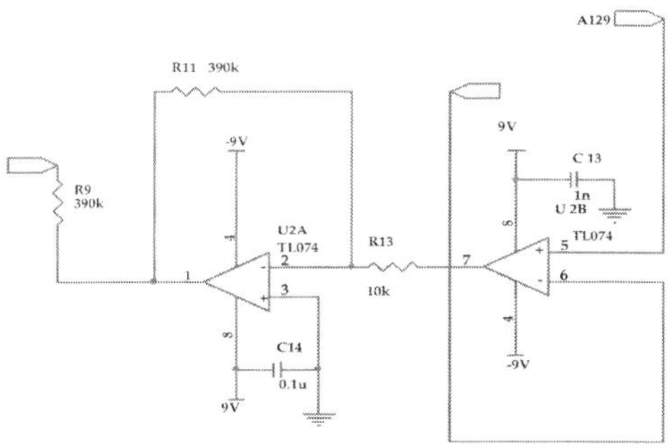

Figure 6.23. The modifications made to the circuit right leg ECG shown in the schematic diagram (*Source: self-made or CC-BY license*).

Similarly, an integrating circuit (Figure 6.24) was used to decrease the offset voltage at the output of instrumentation amplifier to prevent the device from saturation. This circuit was designed taking into account the highest expected frequency, i.e., 500 Hz, taking 10 samples. The values of R and C were obtained as follows [1]:

$$f = \frac{1}{T}. \ , T = RC .$$

$$\frac{1}{50} = RC = 0.2 \approx (270k\Omega)(0.1uF)$$

Finally, the last amplification stage preamp is provided by a TL074 operational amplifier in noninverting configuration (Figure 6.25); then calculate the resistance is to obtain the desired gain [1] 9.6.

$$G = \frac{R6}{R5} + 1$$

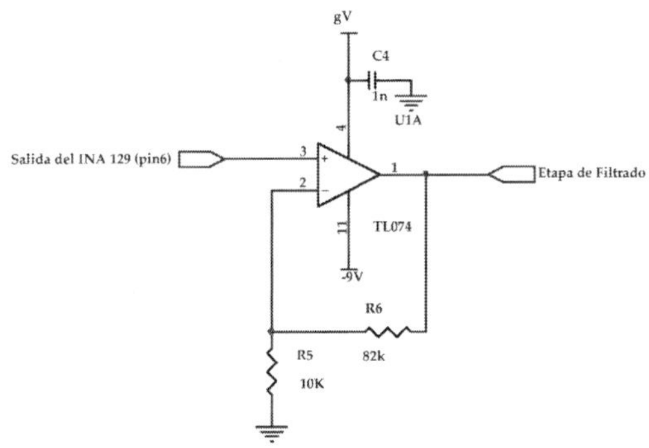

Figure 6.24. Schematic circuit no inverting stage preamp.

Figure 6.26 shows the schematic diagram of the preamplifier, whose output is connected directly to the filtering step.

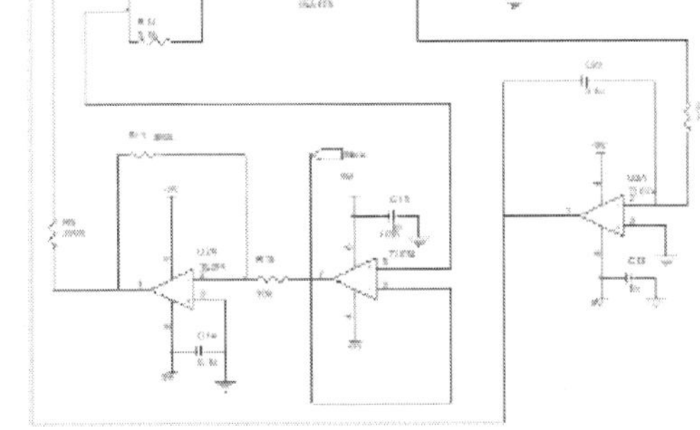

Figure 6.25. TL074 operational amplifier in noninverting configuration (*Source: self-made or CC-BY license*).

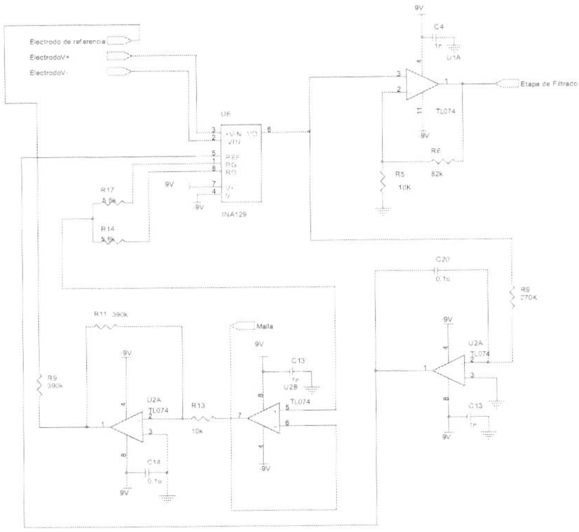

Figure 6.26. Schematic diagram of the preamplifier stage, (*Source: self-made or CC-BY license*).

6.5.3. Stage Filtering

In the pre-amplification, the signal from the electrodes is obtained by differentially instrumentation amplifier, which gives a gain of 10; subsequently, a gain of 9.2 is applied by the TL074 operational amplifier. From this point, the signal from the electrodes is ready to be filtered. For filtering stage amplifiers operations Sallen Key filter configuration were used. However there are three configurations quite Sallen Key filter used, these are the Butterworth, Chebyshev, and Bessel [2] configuration, each of which has certain characteristics (Figure 6.27):

- Butterworth filter, this type of filter has a band of smooth passage and a sharp cut. It is also the filter having the flattest response the more it approaches the cutoff frequency, which is why it is called maximally flat.
- Chebyshev filter is filter has the acute response, but some undulations are also generated before reaching the cutoff frequency, these undulations are reduced with increasing filter order.
- Bessel filter, has a constant phase variation.

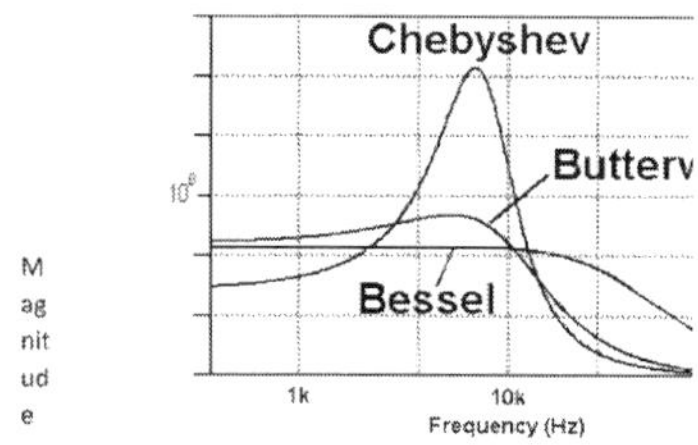

Figure 6.27. Graph magnitude vs. frequency of the different types of filters to a cutoff frequency of 10kHz, (*Source: self-made or CC-BY license*).

Figure 36 shows the magnitude response of the filters, one can observe how Chebyshev filter ripples are reduced and becomes flatter as the response of the Butterworth filter.

Given the characteristics which the different types of filter were chosen using Butterworth configuration because has a very flat response magnitude and slope downward fast when approaching the cutoff frequency. Figure 6.28 shows the response of a Butterworth filter magnitude varying their order [3].

An active bandpass filter 20 to 500Hz from two active second-order Butterworth filter with classic architecture of Sallen-Key in order to obtain EMG signals, which are in the frequency range generated. The bandpass filter was designed in cascade, i.e., first a high pass filter is presented letting frequencies higher than 20Hz and out of this, a lowpass to prevent passage of frequencies above 500Hz filter is connected. In the Figure 6.23, we see that the variations are not significant after the order 1, it is for this reason was chosen to construct the second-order active filter.

To design the high pass filter with cutoff frequency (fc) at 20 Hz of Sallen Key the following formula [3] was used:

$$f_c = \frac{1}{2\pi RC} \qquad usando\, C = 0.1uf \ y \ f_c = 20$$

$$(20)2\pi C = \frac{1}{R} \qquad R \approx 82k\Omega$$

As a second-order Butterworth configuration desired, the filter should have a gain of approximately 1.58 [3], wherein R2 is grounded and the resistance R1 is connecting the non-inverting output with the amplifier output.

$$G = \frac{R2}{R1} + 1$$

Taking the following values of R, we have:

$R2 = 33k$. $R1 = 56kG = \frac{R2}{R1} + 1 = 1.589$ .The lowpass filter design was performed as foows:

$$f_c = \frac{1}{2\pi RC} \quad usando\, C = 0.1uf \; y \; f_c = 500$$

$$(500)2\pi(0.1u) = \frac{1}{R} \qquad R \approx 3.3k\Omega$$

Just as in the high pass filter, the low pass filter (Figure 6.29) has Butterworth configuration so that the gain values are similar to the high pass filter [3]. Figure 36hows the complete filter.

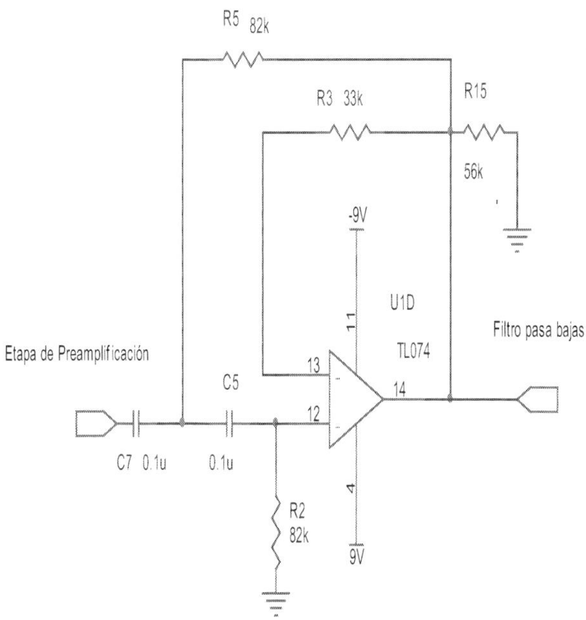

Figure 6.28. Schematic diagram of high pass filter 20Hz, (*Source: self-made or CC-BY license*).

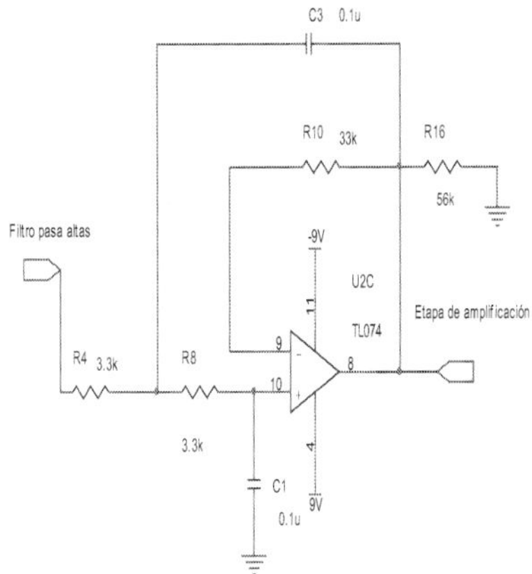

Figure 6.29. Schematic diagram lowpass filter 500Hz, (*Source: self-made or CC-BY license*).

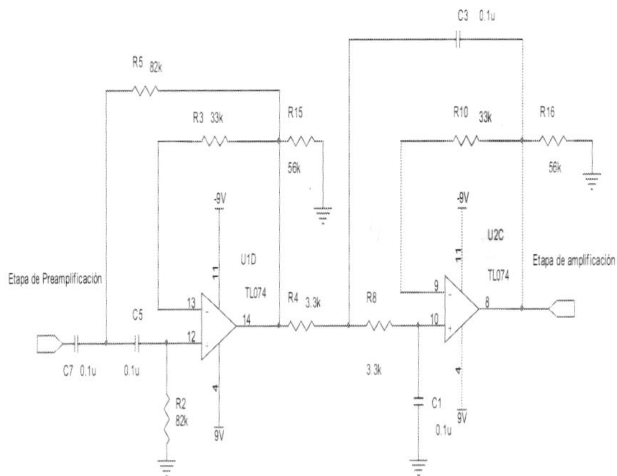

Figure 6.30. Schematic diagram of the bandpass filter 20–500Hz, (*Source: self-made or CC-BY license*).

6.5.4. Final Amplifier Stage

This step is intended to stabilize and amplify the filtered signal by a factor of 9.2 Figure 6.31. The calculation of the values of resistors shown below [1]:

$$G = \frac{R6}{R7} + 1., \qquad R6 = 82k R7 = 10k G = \frac{R6}{R7} + 1 = 9.2.$$

6 CHAPTER

DESIGN AND CONSTRUCTION OF A SYSTEM FOR DETECTING ELECTROMYO-GRAPHIC SIGNALS USING NEURAL NETWORKS

CONTENTS

Biomedical Engineering is a branch of the exact sciences including the study, development, and innovation of technologies for medical, therapy or rehabilitation and management techniques hospital resources. It is in this discipline that is immersed in the development of myoelectric interfaces; a myoelectric interface is an electronic device that uses biological signals produced by the body's muscles, which are processed by electronic circuits and translated to recreate the action of some functional members. Today the development of these devices is increasing, and it already uses not only focuses on the development of therapeutic applications and rehabilitation, as in the case of myoelectric prostheses, which are used to replace the loss of a member, mainly arms, hands or legs. These new trends are developing myoelectric bordering interfaces for everyday use, whether to facilitate daily living or for recreation and entertainment uses; for example the use of myoelectric devices or video games in the near future replace output input devices like a PC mouse or keyboard.

Because of this arises the idea of developing a robust interface able to monitor the actions produced by muscle group to subsequently have a final application in the field of intelligent prostheses. This book presents the design and construction of an interface that processes the myoelectric signals for different muscle groups, which can be used to build self-adjusting prosbook interfaces for performing tasks without direct contact by the operator or simulation systems and 3D animation.

Electricity is present in many forms in nature, so that the human body is no exception, where you will find small electrical impulses through which carry out important functions in the body: heartbeat, breathing, thinking the phenomenon of sight etc. One of the first to contribute in the field of electrical activity in the body was Luigi Galvani [18], who in 1786 discovered animal electricity at one end of a frog by passing electric current in the nerves of the limb and noticed that producing a movement in response to electrical stimulation. The functions performed by the human body are conducted through electrical pulses, these pulses are the result of the electrochemical action of certain types of cells, which generate the potential difference by ionized particles such as potassium, calcium ions, and depolarization of their cell membranes [2]. Many of these potential exchanges take place in the brain, which sends the order as electicos impulses which are transported to another part of the body through the nerves [2]. The nervous system is divided into central nervous system and peripheral nervous system; central nervous system consists of the brain and spinal cord, while the peripheral is made the peripheral nerves and motor terminals [4]. The basic unit of the

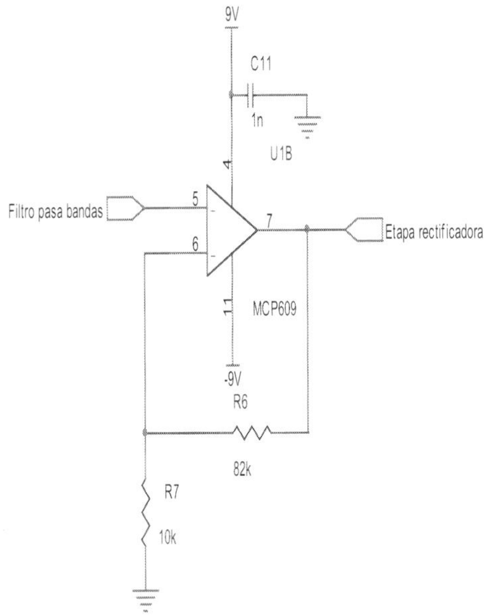

Figure 6.31. Schematic final amplifier in noninverting configuration, (*Source: self-made or CC-BY license*).

6.5.5. Stage half-Wave Rectification

A potential single action (Figure 6.32) consists of a signal with a positive component and a negative is for this reason that the method of half-wave rectification is chosen, thus avoid taking the negative components and only take positive per action potential [18].

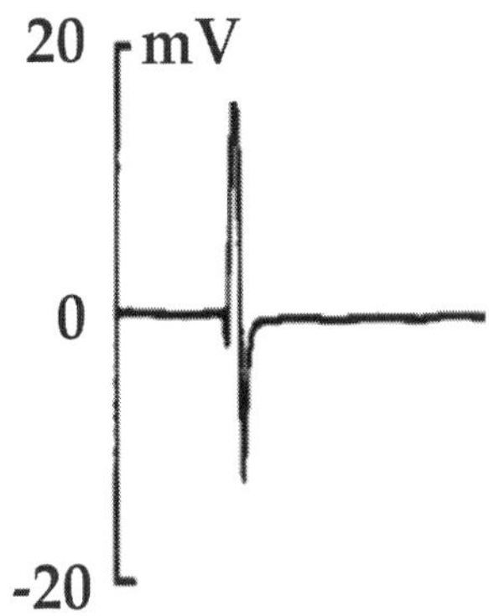

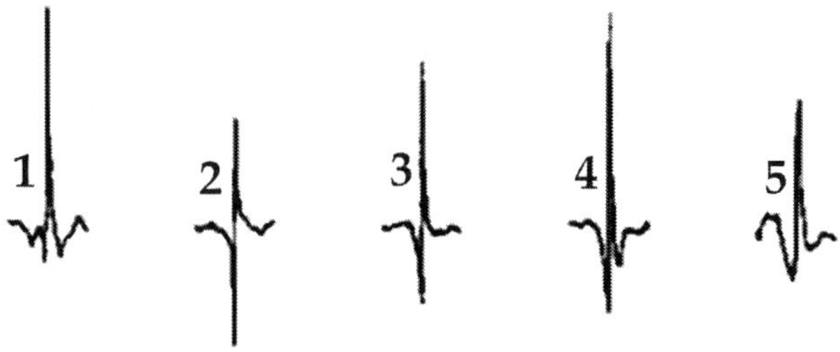

Figure 6.32. Different potential from the UM, (*Source: self-made or CC-BY license*).

The rectifier circuit used is a half-wave rectifier of accuracy, also known as super diode [1] (Figure 6.33).

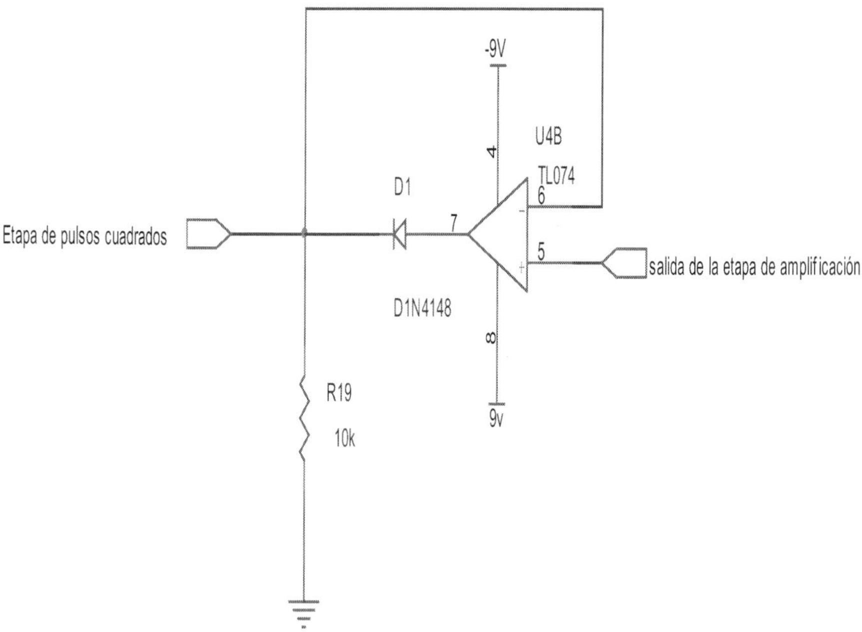

Figure 6.33. Schematic half wave rectifier precisión, (*Source: self-made or CC-BY license*).

6.5.6. Stage Square Pulses

With the rectified signal, it proceeds to use a non-inverting comparator circuit; This circuit has the function of transforming information duration (seconds) action potential UM to a square pulse with the same duration. This process is just making a comparison of the rectified averaging the same signal; thus, when an action potential is present, the signal exceed the average thereof and comparator triggers a square pulse, in this case, the pulse generated will have a value that will go from 0 volts to the saturation voltage positive in this case is 9V; comparator for a specific amplifier was used to perform the function (LM311) [16]. To perform the signal averaging an array of capacitor and resistor whose values were calculated experimentally constructed. Figure 6.34 shows the schematic diagram of the circuit generating pulses. Finally, we can see the schematic diagram of the entire system (Figure 6.35).

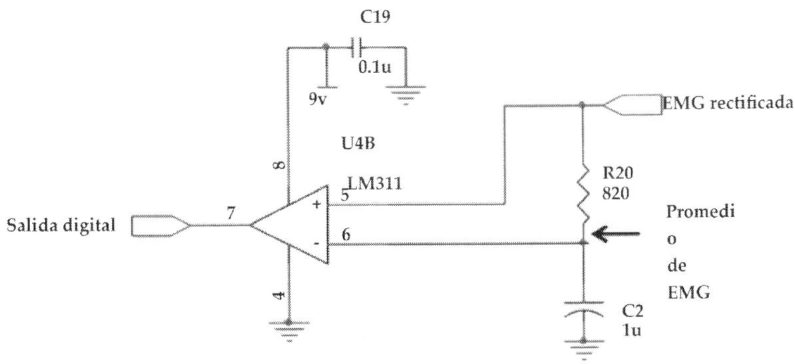

Figure 6.34. Schematic diagram of the comparator circuit generating square pulses, (*Source: self-made or CC-BY license*).

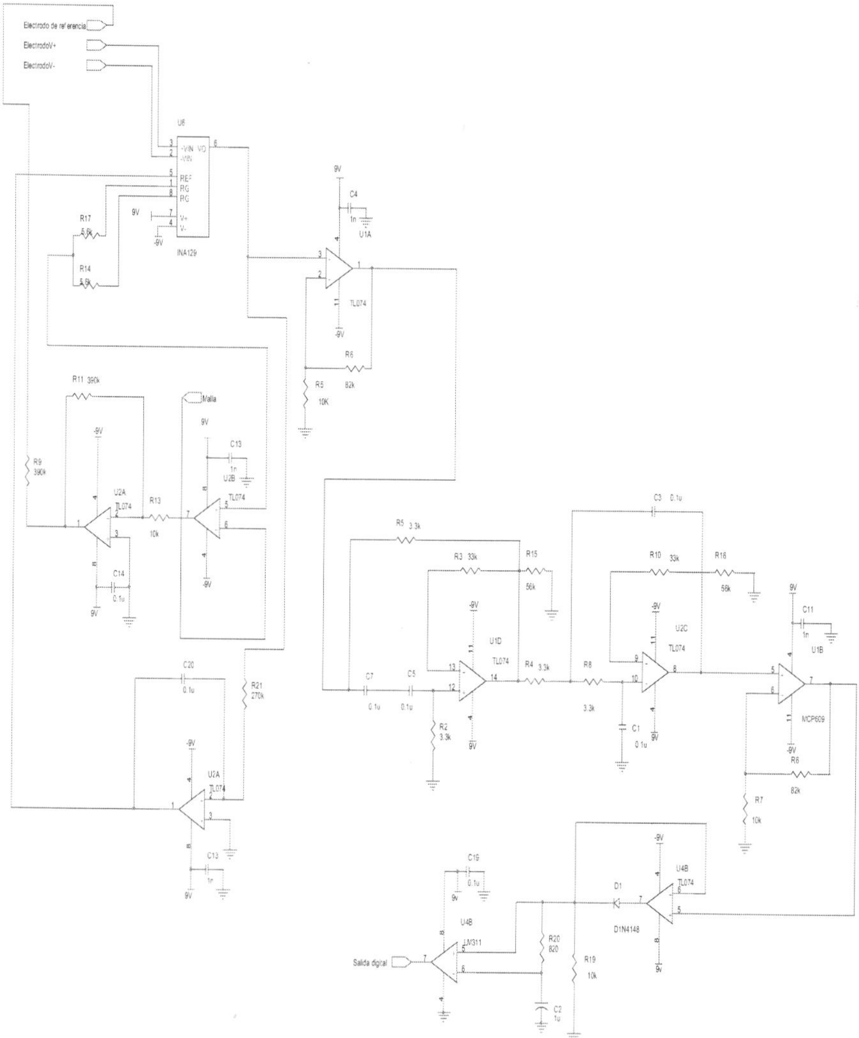

Figure 6.35. Schematic diagram of the entire system for the acquisition of EMG signals with bipolar sources, (*Source: self-made or CC-BY license*).

PCB design circuit this first prototype was developed with the Proteus program. It was developed in several printed circuit boards (Figure 46) because it was an experimental prototype; on the main board is the pre-amplification, filtering, and final amplification, on another card are the feedback stage, another integrator circuit and in another step of half-wave rectification and the stage of square pulses (Figure 6.36).

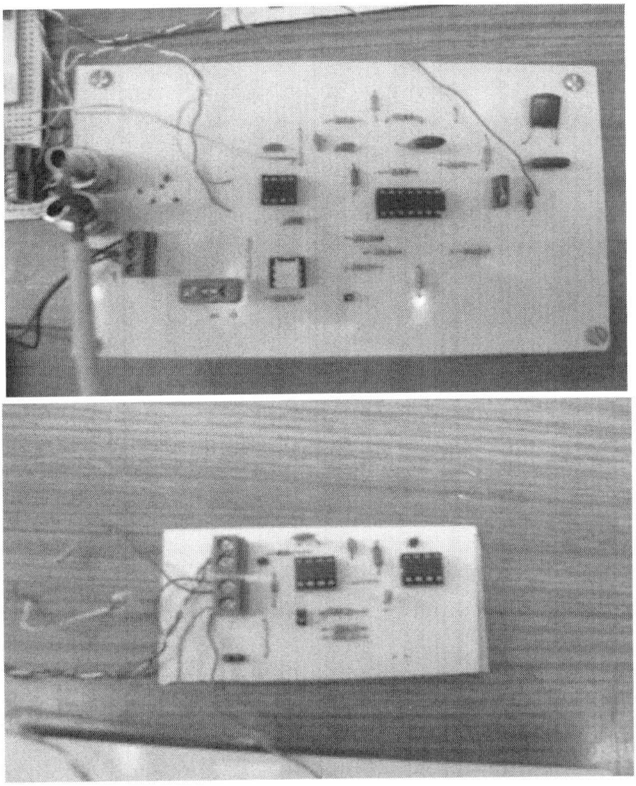

Figure 6.36. Approach to the main board and card rectification with square pulses, (*Source: self-made or CC-BY license*).

Once the prototype working, it was necessary to take samples and keep records captured by the system; in the first instance could be observed potential on the oscilloscope, however the need arises to have the records of these potential on the computer to plot them and compare them later records is why a very powerful tool used in the field electronic instrumentation, virtual instrumentation. Virtual instrumentation is a way of making measurements and signal processing without the need for hardware with which it normally would in an electronics laboratory; is a software which can perform processing both analog and digital signals without the need for team physically, but rather it is "virtual" way, you can program all the features needed. This concept was created with the idea of using the PC to make measurements, e.g., temperature, pressure, etc. Virtual instrumentation is a layer of software and hardware that allow the user to use custom tools tailored to the user.

In our case, virtual instrumentation was used to digitize the potential EMG and save them for later plotting them. For this task use the LabView software from National Instruments. To perform the task of digitizing the data EMG-USB-6009 acquisition card NI National Instruments was used. The NI USB-6009 card is configured to have a sampling rate of 10kHz, taking a 5V voltage scale maximum and acquisition mode that was set up to DAQ was referencing.

Subsequently, it developed a small application in LabView to graph and save data acquisition by pressing a button (Figure 6.37).

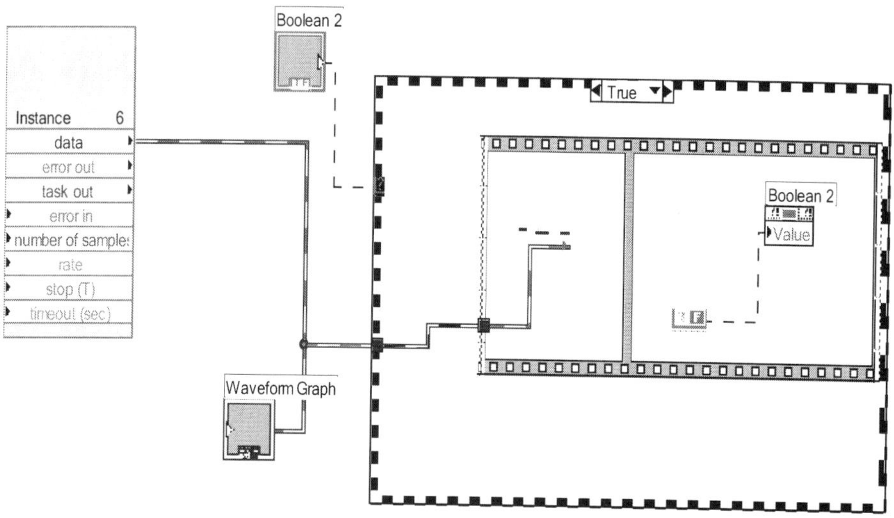

Figure 6.37. Program LabView to keep records of EMG.

6.5.7. Results

With the prototype connected to a voluntary EMG activity logs they were made, and by the data acquisition card from National, Instruments was possible analog-digital conversion of these signals. Recorded movements were smooth and strong bending. Figure 6.38 shows a record corresponding to movement of soft flex, 1000 samples were captured at 1-second availing card data acquisition NI USB-6009.

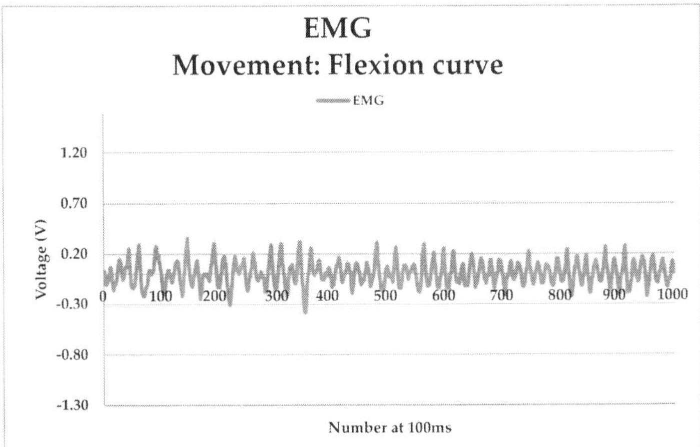

Figure 6.38. Registration EMG signal. The record corresponds to the movement of soft flex. Records corresponding to 1000 samples taken at a frequency of 10kHz, corresponding capture 100ms, (*Source: self-made or CC-BY license*).

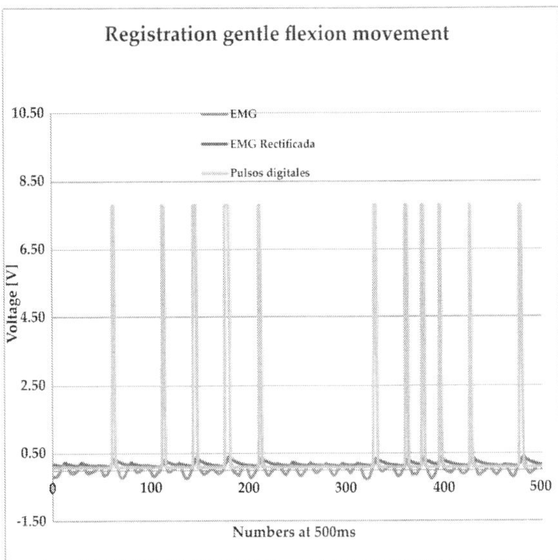

Figure 6.39. Registration gentle flexion movement. The graph shows the pure EMG signal (blue) is observed, the EMG rectified signal (red) and the square pulses generated by each action potential (green), (*Source: self-made or CC-BY license*).

Figure 6.39 shows a graph of the same data recorded corresponding to movement of soft flex, showing 500 samples taken at 500ms. In this graph you can see the signal EMG, EMG signal rectified and square pulses generated by the comparator circuit; you can clearly see how the square pulses correspond exactly to the action potentials.

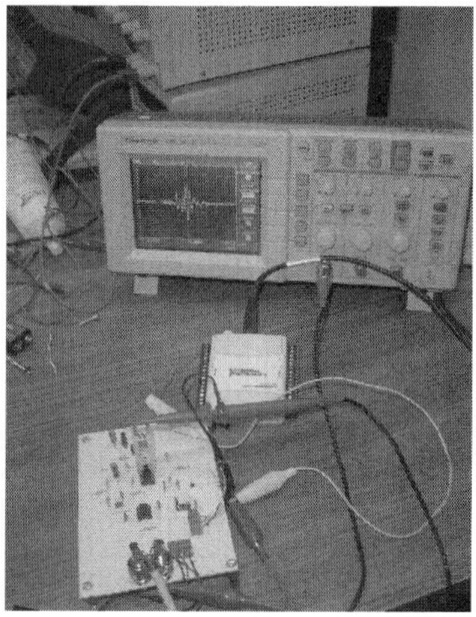

Figure 6.40. Register strong bending movement of the arm during 100ms, (*Source: self-made or CC-BY license*).

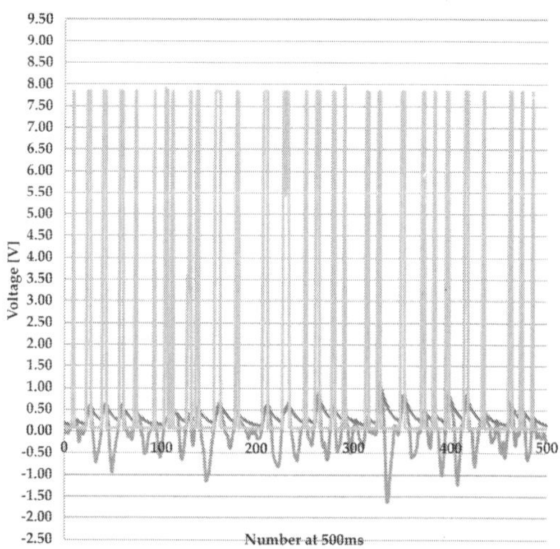

Figure 6.41. Registration of strong bending motion. The graph shows the pure EMG signal (blue) is observed, the EMG rectified signal (red) and the square pulses generated by each action potential (green), (*Source: self-made or CC-BY license*).

Figure 6.40 shows records EMG activity corresponding bending force by arm biceps muscle. It shows that this signal is greater in amplitude graphed in Figure 49. The image in Figure 6.41 shows a screenshot of EMG made with the oscilloscope during strong bending arm. The graph of Figure 53 shows the pulses generated by the comparator circuit during strong bending movement, this movement generates more population activity action potential and increasing the amplitude of these potential. Similarly, note that the square pulses coincide in time with the action potentials.

6.5.8. Design and Construction of the Prototype Acquisition Single Channel EMG LVTTL

This prototype has several improvements over the previous one is the use of powerful integrated circuits, Tables 6.2–6.4 show a comparison of the most significant characteristics of the chips used in the construction of previous prototype and chips used in the new prototype.

Table 6.2. Comparative Table of Instrumentation Amplifiers Used in the Prototypes

	INA129 (bipolar source prototype)	INA326 (Prototype LVTTL)	Units
CMRR	120	114	dB
Offset Voltage	50	100	Microvolts
Input impedance	1010 || 2	1010 || 2	Ω || pF
Power Supplies	± 6.25 to ± 18	+5.5 +6.7 to	V
Noise at 1kHz	8	33	nV / $\sqrt{Hz}$.
Bias current	5	± 2	nA
Single power supply	No	Yes	

Table 6.3. Comparative.Tablas of Used Operational Amplifiers

	TL074 (Bipolar source prototype)	OPA4376 (Prototype LVTTL)	Units
Offset Voltage	50	5	Microvolts
CMRR	85	90	dB
Power Supplies	± 18	to 5.5	V
Noise at 1kHz	15	0.8	nV / $\sqrt{Hz}$.

Table 6.4. Main Characteristics of the Operational Amplifiers Used in the Auto Zero LVTTL Prototype

	OPA2333 (Prototype LVTTL)	OPA2335 (Prototype LVTTL)	Units
Offset Voltage	6. 3	5	Microvolts
CMRR	130	130	dB
Power Supplies	6.7 5.5	6.7 5.5	V

One of the more significant changes whichccount prototype LVTTL regarding Bipolar, is the use of a single power supply, which is 3.3V unlike feeding previously used (± 9V), hence the LVTTL name (Low Voltage Transistor-Transistor Logic). Because EMG potentials have positive and negative components, it is necessary to handle two voltage levels, one more positive and a less positive. For this reason a reference or "virtual ground" making an active voltage divider was implemented. This "virtual ground" will have the value of half the power supply 3.3V (1.65 V) and this reference voltage is mounted EMG signal while the power supplies of the chips will be 0V for V- and 3.3V to V +.

An issue to consider is the consumption and the life of the power supply to be used to feed the system; in our case, the system must be able to run on batteries either Li-Ion, coal or nickel metal hydride. When working with batteries must take into account some aspects such should be maintained at a voltage supply as invariant as possible. This is because the A/D converter shall refer conversion values the power supply and if these vary over time, wrong data will have to complete the conversion. The solution was to incorporate a charge pump circuit which takes as input the voltage from the batteries; these circuits are responsible for maintaining a voltage at a fixed level regardless of change of the power supply, i.e., if the voltage is above the desired value (3.3V) then it acts as a regulator and reduces the voltage to 3.3 V while if encentra at a level below 3.3, for example, 2V then acts as a step-up circuit which raises the voltage to 3.3V desired; the circuit used to perform this task was the REG-711 [15] of Texas Instruments, which can handle input voltages of 1.8V to 5.5V having as output a value of 3.3V. Figure 6.42 shows the schematic diagram of the voltage divider and the active charge pump circuit. 3V whereas if encentra at a level below 3.3, for example, 2V then acts as a step-up circuit which raises the voltage to 3.3V desired; the circuit used to perform this task was the REG-711 [15] of Texas Instruments, which can handle input voltages of 1.8V to 5.5V having as output a value of 3.3V.

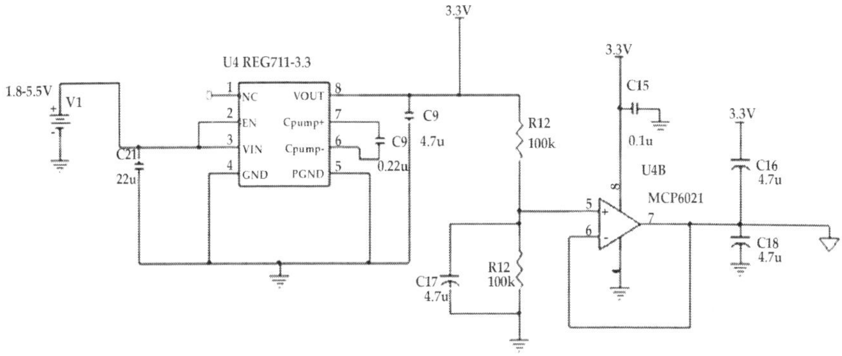

Figure 6.42. Schematic diagram for regulating the input voltage and the reference voltage setting or "virtual ground," (*Source: self-made or CC-BY license*).

6.5.9. Electrodes

The changes in the used type of electrodes were made above the silver electrodes of silver (Ag/AgCl) chloride were used. These pads are disposable and come with a layer of conductive gel ensures better contact between the metal and the skin. This disadvantage this type electrode is limited use because they are used only once and use them for a long period of time conducive to the shore bondable car with that account lose its grip and this fall the body, limiting, and records; For this reason dry [18] surface electrodes were designed stainless steel. This electrodes have a rectangular shape whose dimensions.

The material used for the construction was stainless steel; Rectangles 1.5 cm x 1.2 cm were cut from a sheet of stainless steel of 30 cm x 30 cm. We aimed sanding and clean the face of the conductive plate would be in contact with the skin, Figure 6.43, while on the other side a screw of stainless steel in the future the electrode can be screwed to a plate was welded circuit where the instrumentation amplifier Figure 6.44 would be located.

Before reaching the final dimensions (1.5 cm x 1.2 cm), tests with rectangles of various sizes were mainly sought to make smaller the area of the conductive plate; however, tests with plates with smaller dimensions 1 cm were not encouraging because the EMG signal could not be recorded.

In total there were three electrodes which were built, the investor electrode, the non-inverting and reference. These electrodes were mounted in a band to fit around the spleen

The separation distance between the inverter and noninverting electrodes was 1 cm, was treated using the spacing as small as possible, because in this way a better selectivity is obtained [5]. Modifications as to the location of the reference electrode, which in the earlier prototype was placed in the wrist, this time was placed in the center of the triceps muscle, were also made.

Due to the change of the distance inter-electrode is necessary to change the gains chain cascade, this is because the surface EMG signal depends inter-electrode distance; a greater separation distance greater signal amplitude and smaller amplitude smaller distance; however, if this distance exceeds either too large or too small will result in signal distortion or disappearance thereof. The inter-distance electrode previously used was 2 cm and the current is 1 cm, however, these variables (distance interelectrode and EMG amplitude) are not directly proportional, that is why the new chain gains was calculated as experimental.

6.5.10. Pre Amplification Stage

In the pre-amplification INA326 instrumentation amplifier I was used. This amplifier has a few differences in their internal structure, with which the method of calculating the gain changes significantly (Figure 6.43).

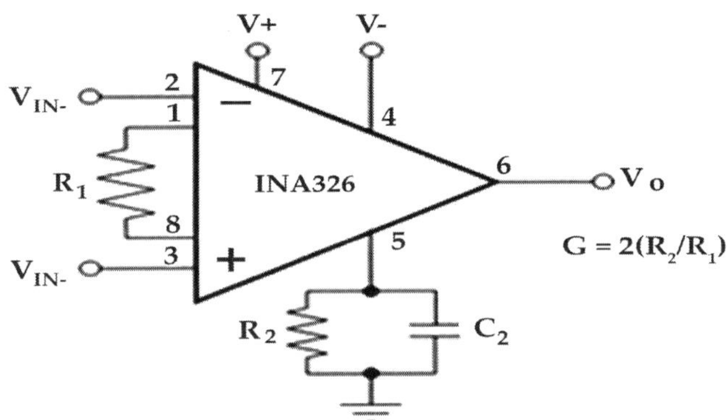

Figure 6.43. Method of calculating the gain changes (*Source: self-made or CC-BY license*).

Table 6.5 shows the values of resistors in parallel with the recommended by the manufacturer to achieve the desired gain capacitor, it is worth mentioning that values change whether a unipolar or bipolar configuration is used.

In this case as the desired gain is 10, and the configuration is unipolar, the values of R1 = 40K and R2 taken || C2 = 200k || 0.5nF.

In the same way as in the prototype bipolar source, right leg circuit such as that proposed in the INA129 data sheet [8] was included; with the only difference that instead of taking land 0V reference the "virtual land" was taken as the new reference; In addition, instead of using the TL074 amplifiers car amplifiers OPA2333 zero family were used as recommended by the data sheet. The circuit schematic of modified right channel shown in Figure 6.44.

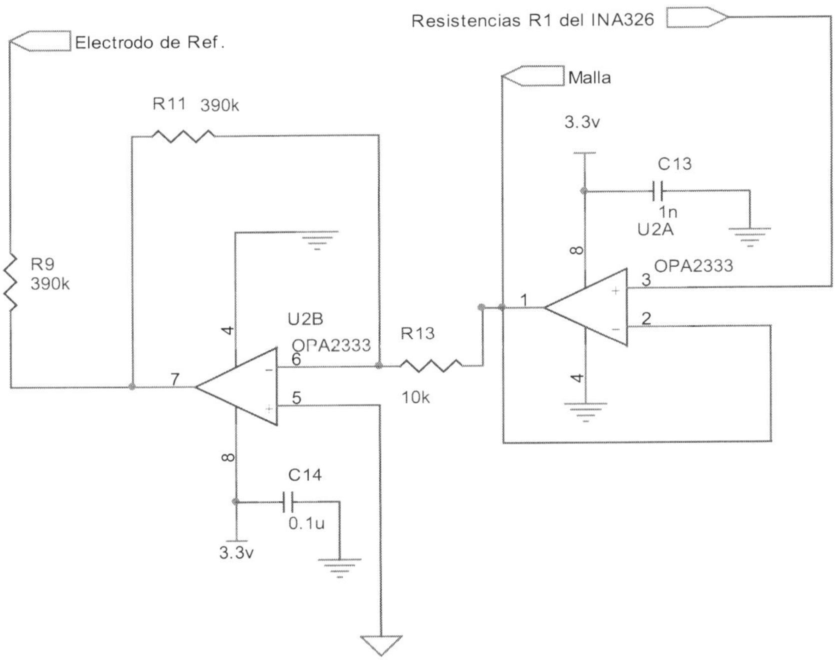

Figure 6.44. Schematic circuit right leg for the prototype 3.3V, (*Source: self-made or CC-BY license*).

The output referred to as mesh shield is connected with the cable which has electrodes; as mentioned in the bipolar design prototype, the mesh is intended to maintain low levels of leakage. The shielded cable used was one with three inner conductors one for the non-inverting electrode, an inverter and one for the reference electrode; this wire turn has a DB9 connector which is used to connect to the acquisition card in which the instrumentation amplifier and other circuitry is located. Figure 6.39 shows the cable used for connection of the electrodes, while Figure 6.45 shows the connection of the lead wires of the electrodes and mesh with DB9 connector.

The integrator circuit used in the prototype bipolar source in order to adapt to the virtual ground is suitably modified. The values of capacitor and resistance maintained their value. The operational amplifier used was the OPA2335 [11] (Figure 6.46). Calculating resistances below, taking a value of 10 samples of the signal with the highest frequency component of the EMG signal (500Hz).

$$f = \frac{1}{T}\ ,\ T = RC$$

$$\frac{1}{50} = RC = 0.2 \approx (270k\Omega)(0.1uF)$$

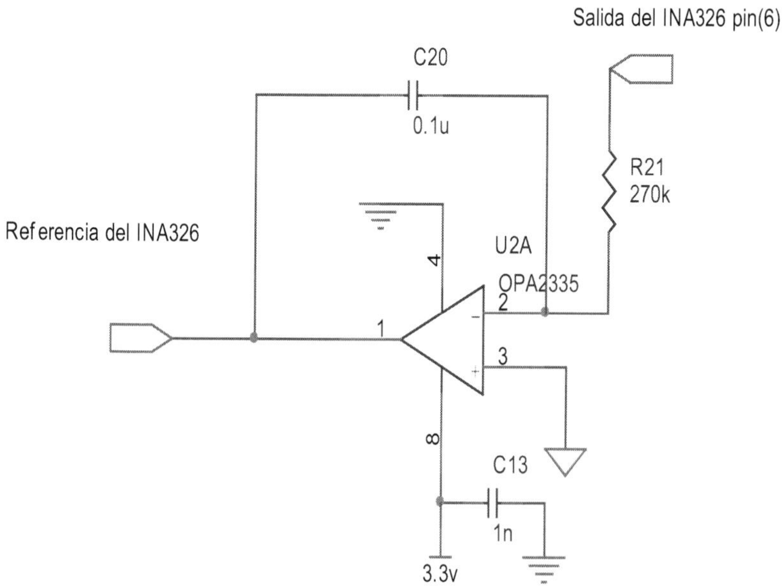

Figure 6.45. Schematic diagram of the integrator circuit with the changes necessary to work at 3.3V using OPA2335, (*Source: self-made or CC-BY license*).

Immediately after the instrumentation amplifier, an amplification step with a value of 11 was placed, the schematic is shown in Figure 6.45. Use one OPA4376 [12] amplifier in noninverting configuration. The calculation of the resistance shown below:

$$G = \frac{R6}{R5} + 1 = 11$$

.

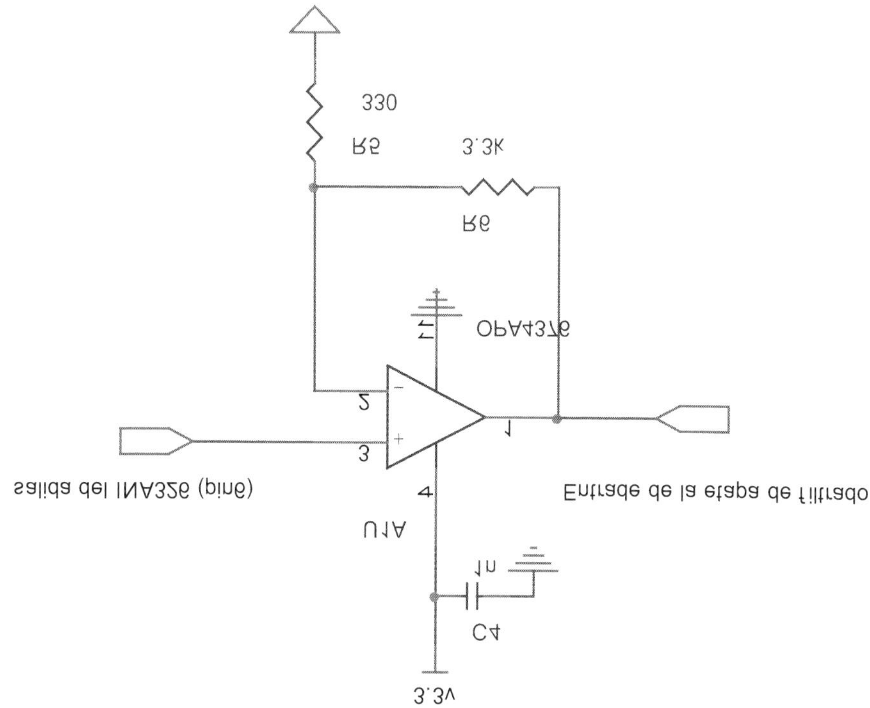

Figure 6.46. Schematic diagram of the output amplification circuit INA326 and before entering the filtering step, (*Source: self-made or CC-BY license*).

Figure 6.46 shows the schematic diagram of the pre-amplification prototype 3.3 Volts. Now all references amplifiers are connected to the virtual ground.

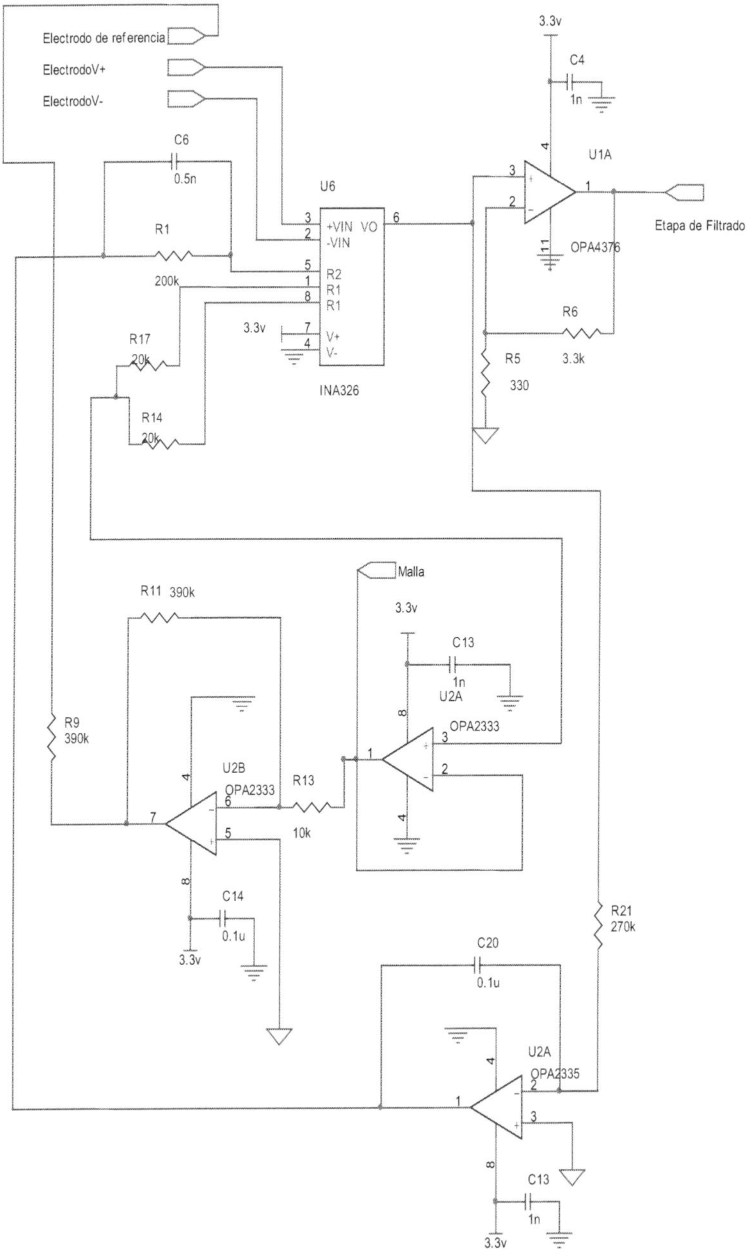

Figure 6.47. Schematic diagram of the pre-amplification, (*Source: self-made or CC-BY license*).

6.5.11. Stage Filtering

For the filtering step the same approach was followed in the previous prototype; EMG components are considered with frequencies of 20 to 500 Hz only the reference signal change as it is now mounted on the "virtual ground." For filtering one high pass filter (20 Hz) (Figure 6.56) followed by a lowpass (500Hz), filter (Figure 6.48) was used to form the bandpass filter 20–500 Hz. Similarly, the filters are second order Butterworth [3] configuration:

$$G = \frac{R2}{R1} + 1$$

Taking the following values of R, we have:

$$R2 = 33k \qquad R1 = 56k G = \frac{R2}{R1} + 1 = 1.589$$

Calculating the values of high pass filter [3] shown below:

$$f_c = \frac{1}{2\pi RC} \qquad C = 0.1uf\ y\ f_c = 20$$

$$(20) * 2\pi * C = \frac{1}{R} \qquad R \approx 82k\Omega$$

The design of the lowpass filter [3] was performed as follows:

$$f_c = \frac{1}{2\pi RC} \qquad C = 0.1uf\ y\ f_c = 500$$

$$(500)2\pi(0.1u) = \frac{1}{R} \qquad R \approx 3.3k\Omega$$

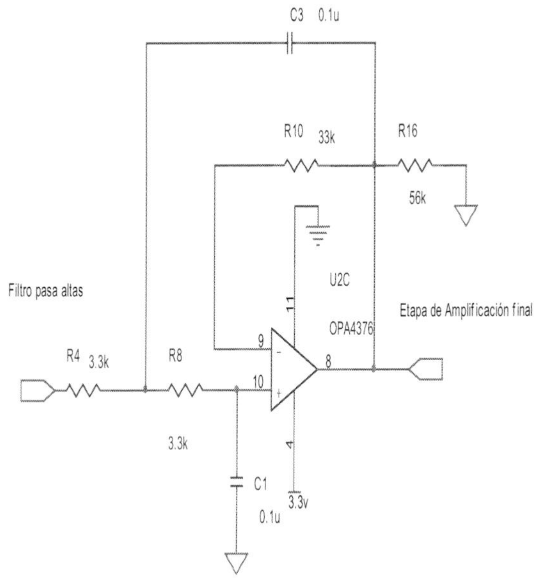

Figure 6.48. Schematic pass filter 500Hz Butterworth second order high setting, (*Source: self-made or CC-BY license*).

The complete schematic diagram of the band-pass filter 20–500Hz shown in Figure 6.49.

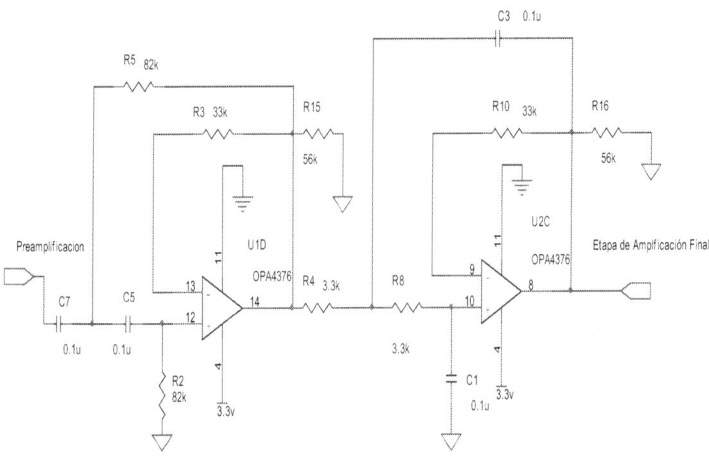

Figure 6.49. Schematic full bandpass filter of 20- 500Hz (*Source: self-made or CC-BY license*).

6.5.12. Final Amplifier Stage

The gain of the amplifier stage (Figure 6.50) was 8, using a non-inverting amplifier; calculating resistors to set the gain is as follows:

$$G = \frac{R6}{R7} + 1$$

$$usando\ R6 = 3.3k, \quad R7 = 470$$

$$G = \frac{R6}{R7} + 1 = \frac{3.3k}{470} + 1 = 7 + 1 = 8$$

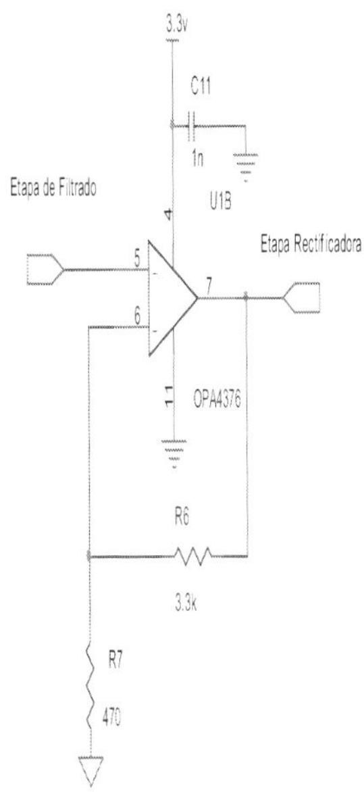

Figure 6.50. Schematic diagram of final amplifier in noninverting configuration, (*Source: self-made or CC-BY license*).

5.6.13. Stage Half-Wave Rectification

After being filtered and amplified EMG signal, it proceeds to the step of half-wave rectification; Figure 6.51 at this stage amplifier autozero OPA2335 used; the output of this stage is connected to the stage or directly to digital pulses in digital-analog converter.

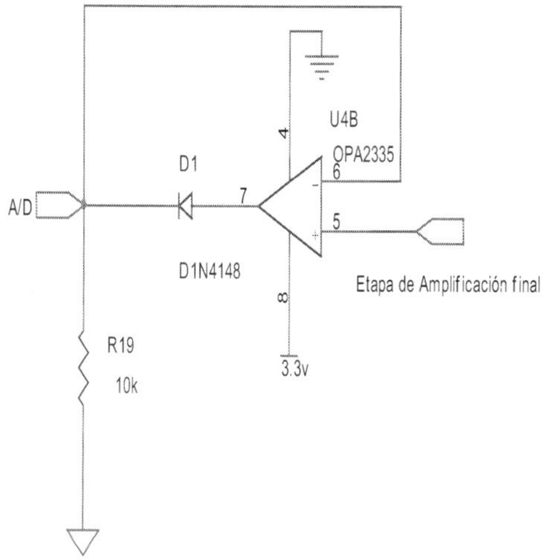

Figure 6.51. Schematic diagram of circuit half-wave rectification, (*Source: self-made or CC-BY license*).

6.5.14. Digital Pulses

The digital pulse stage was added in order to obtain information from the EMG signals in digital form. At this stage, the generated digital pulses have an amplitude of 3.3V, so it can be interpreted by any work with LVTTL chip technology. A comparator circuit TLV302 Texas Instruments was used for comparison between EMG signal rectified and the average thereof, thus when a potential of a motor unit present, the EMG signal rectified overtake its average and therefore the comparator will change its current state (0V) by the state of saturation 3.3V positive (noninverting comparator), thus a square pulse of duration equal to the generated action potential UM.

However this output is serial, and is a continuous pulse train, and for future application with an artificial Neural Network, output is required in parallel.

Artificial Neural Networks are built imitating possible architecture of a biological Neural Network, this is "neurons" that are arranged in layers, connections or "synapses" between neurons and these connections may be excitatory or inhibitory used.

And an artificial Neural Network has n number of inputs, number of intermediate layers kr m number of outputs (Figure 6.52).

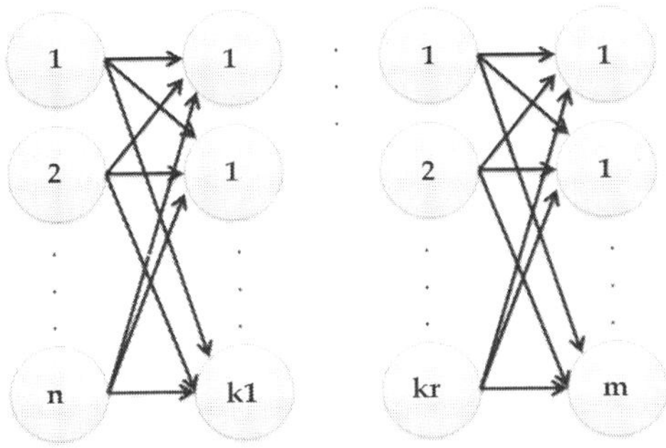

Figure 6.52. Representation of the artificial neural network of n inputs and 1 output.

One way to create compatibility between the digital pulse trains and the input of a Neural Network is using a switching circuit (shift register) [23]. These circuits perform the conversion of a TTL signal serial input to the same TTL but parallel (Figure 6.53) value, thus we could use a circuit of this type and its serial input connect the output of digital pulses later have the parallel output. However, a difficulty arises; circuits shift registers require an internal or external clock for conversion; thus will require a circuit operating at a frequency of 10 kHz at least as the higher frequency EMG is 500Hz, thereby to deliver sufficient output to parallel data 20 is time would.

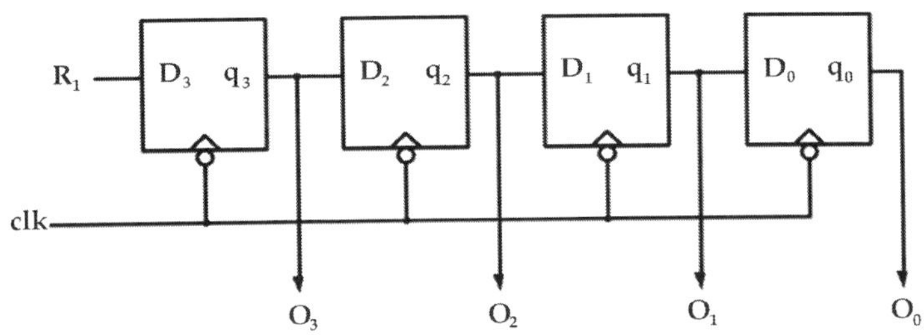

Figure 6.53. Circuit serial to parallel shift with 4 outputs, (*Source: self-made or CC-BY license*).

The input circuit Serial-parallel shift register several difficulties, such as finding one that can operate with a frequency of less internal clock when 10kHz; and is compatible with LVTTL logic, it is for this reason that in developing the system for acquisition of EMG was not taken into account this circuit; instead we chose to use a digital-analog converter.

6.5.15. Analog to Digital Conversion

With EMG signal rectified, it proceeds to step digital-analog conversion. To select an A/D right was necessary to ask yourself questions such as: What sampling rate?

Because the largest components in frequency EMG signal occurring around the 500Hz and the sampling theorem Nyquist, a converter to sample the signal at a frequency at least twice the highest harmonic is required (500Hz) then it requires at least a sampling frequency of 1 kHz.

In the market there are many digital-analog converters; however, these circuits require complementary components such oscillators, voltage reference circuits, regulators etc. Then there are the internal digital-analog converters microcontrollers, these circuits have the advantage of being configured by software and have much more versatility at least for this particular application; As for bits of resolution, these converters offer us 8 to 10 bits.

One of the main advantages offered by the internal A/D of a microcontroller is able to present the value of the conversion output pins are there in the micro, in this way we obtain the parallel input requiring artificial Neural Network.

Internal digital-analog converter is a microcontroller Microchip PIC, which was used for the conversion PIC16F687 [7] (Figure 6.54) and was fed with a voltage (VDD) 3.3V. The main features of this microcontroller are shown in Table 6.5.

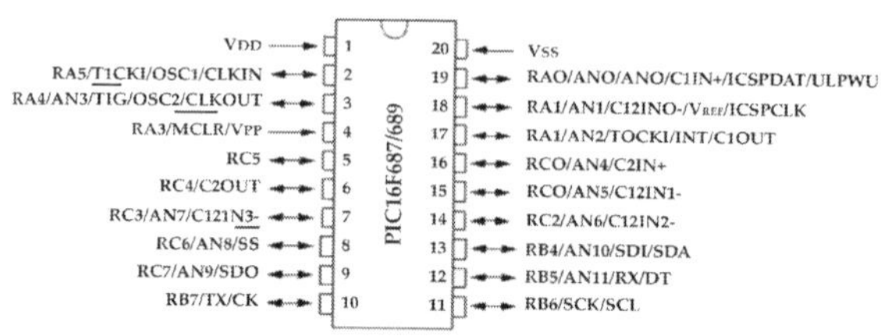

Figure 6.54. Diagram pin PIC16F687, (*Source: self-made or CC-BY license*).

Table 6.5. Main Features of the PIC16F687

Features PIC16F687
8MHz internal oscillator – 32kHz
External oscillator 4MHz – 20MHz

Operating voltage of 6.0V to 5.5V
12 channel A/D converter with 10-bit resolution
RS-232
17 pin input/output and one pin as input only

He is having chosen the microcontroller attention on the characteristics of the A/D converter, mainly in the sampling frequency conversion bits and focused.

First, you must set the reference voltage for conversion, based on this voltage signal EMG rectified which has 1V average amplitude, thereby a voltage value higher than 1V far reference is needed will be measured, but remember EMG signal that is mounted on 1.65V, therefore, really need a voltage greater than 6.65V. The PIC16F687 gives the option of choosing an external reference voltage (which should be placed in the PIN RA1) or using the PIC supply voltage (3.3V); so to save extra components will be preferred to use VDD (3.3V) as the reference voltage for the A/D converter. Recall that in this design the voltage 3.3V is provided by a charge pump circuit which is responsible for maintaining always fixed voltage level (regulates).

To perform its functions, the A/D needs a clock oscillator or by which the sampling frequency is fixed; in the case of A/D PIC16f687 it is possible to choose to use an internal oscillator which works 32kHz to 8MHz or 4MHz oscillator external to 20MHz; however, because the biological signals that are processed are too prone to noise and considering that the external oscillator may interfere with these, is preferred to use the internal oscillator frequency of 8MHz, thus each instruction cycle of the microcontroller only takes 0.5μs. Once chosen the oscillator, the following is to select the sampling rate of the A/D; it will be in proportion to the oscillator frequency (FOSC = 8MHz),

An important point is the time to complete the conversion of a single bit (TAD); as to complete a 10-bit conversion 11 TADs are required.

Table 6.6. Gray Cells Indicate a Value not Recommended

ADC clock	Frequency	Of the device	(FOSC)	Internal oscillator frequency
	20MHz	8MHz	4MHz	1MHz
FOSC/2	100ns (2)	250ns (2)	500ns (2)	6.0μs

FOSC/4	200ns (2)	500ns (2)	1.0μs (2)	4.0μs
FOSC/8	400ns (2)	1.0μs (2)	6.0μs	8.0μs (3)
FOSC/16	800ns (2)	6.0μs	4.0μs	16.0μs (3)
FOSC/32	1.6μs	4.0μs	8.0μs (3)	36.0μs (3)
FOSC/64	3.2μs	8.0μs	16.0μs (3)	64.0μs (3)
FRC	2–6μs (1.4)	2–6μs (1.4)	2–6μs (1.4)	2–6μs (1.4)

Notes (super indexes):

(1): The TAD FCR has a typical time for 4μs VDD> 3.0V (2): These values violate at least TAD required. (3): For faster conversions, select another clock. (4) When the frequency of the device is larger than 1MHz, the FCR is only recommended in the sleep mode.

Because a full 10-bits conversion using the internal oscillator frequency (FOSC/16) typically takes 11 * TAD TAD and for voltages greater than 3.0V takes 2μs, then the full time for conversion of 10bits we take:

$$T_{conversion} = 11 * 2\mu s = 22\mu s$$

This conversion time () is equivalent to a sampling rate: $T_{conversion}$

$$f_{muestreo} = \frac{1}{T_{conversion}} = \frac{1}{22\mu s} = 45.45kHz$$

As the minimum frequency at which we should sample the signal EMG to avoid "aliasing" is 1kHz, and our sampling frequency obtained for the conversion of 10 bits is 45.45kHz, then we can sample the EMG signal without problems.

10-bit conversion is used for digital data, thus 2n–1 have values (1023). Taking into account that the average amplitude of the EMG signal is about 1V and which is mounted on the voltage level of 1.65V (virtual ground), it has a voltage value of 1V + 1.65V = 6.65de average value.

7 CHAPTER

CONCLUSIONS

Based on Neural Networks for the detection of human figures in an imaging system, it is created. This was tested using both images containing persons walking position and opposite, and other objects. Being a prototype system still does not act autonomously, on the other hand, the Neural Network is already functional allowing transport to other teams to start working even if particular needs the system needs another type of training simply requires a lot of images to start training.

The fact that the system works with free software tools that are on different operating systems allows the application can be easily migrated between operating systems. On the other hand, to be a working under the client/server architecture version is possible to work with the server on an operating system with clients in other systems, and through the use of XML messages will allow a future possible work with clients written in different programming languages using a common server.

The method of differentiating the background object being analyzed is very good when it is in a controlled constant illumination but works poorly when shadows are generated or a change in lighting environment. For a future version must be necessary to find a better segmentation method for the time when the application should work autonomously should be done in a very controlled not to allow abrupt changes in the conditions necessary for the optimal work environment.

Working with Neural Networks has proved to be a good option when creating an identifier of features, but has also proven to be very difficult to design choice. Choose the number of entries, the number of neurons in the hidden layer, the training algorithm can be an expensive task. For future applications will be necessary to use other classifiers such as support vector machines that have proven easier to set up and work with fewer parameters and tend to better generalize fewer training data as shown in Ref. [13].

The system has problems with images that generate a string similar to the codes generated by a human silhouette although the image does not have an obvious resemblance to the human figure, for future work must be necessary to review how to counter this problem.

BIBLIOGRAPHY

1. Westerweel, J. (1997). Fundamentals of digital particle image velocimetry. Measurement science and technology, 8(12), 1379.
2. Molina, R., (1998). Introduction to processing and analyzing digital images, Spain: University of Granada.
3. Friedman, M., & Kandel, A., (1999). Introduction to pattern recognition. Statistical, structural, neural and fuzzy logic Approaches, UK: Imperial College Press.
4. Gonzalez, R., & Woods, R., (2002). Digital Image Processing, USA: Prentice Hall, 2002.
5. Gonzalez, R., Woods, R., & Eddins, S., (2003). Digital Image Processing using MATLAB, USA: Prentice Hall.
6. Singh, M., Basu, A., & Mandal, M. K. (2008). Human activity recognition based on silhouette directionality. IEEE transactions on circuits and systems for video technology, 18(9), 1280-1292.
7. Coppin, B., (2004). Artificial Intelligence Illuminated, USA: Jones and Bartlett Publishers.
8. Carter, M., (2007). Minds and Computers, Scotland: Edinburgh University Press Ltd.
9. Verma, B., & Blumenstein, M., (2008). Pattern Recognition Technologies and Applications: Recent Advance, USA: IGI Global.
10. Kasabov, N., (1998). Foundations of Neural Networks, Fuzzy Systems, and Knowledge Engineering, UK: The MIT Press.

11. Valencia, M. J., & Reeds., (2007). "Registration passersby in real time using a machine vision system for a controlled environment," Thesis, UTP.
12. Gopalakrishnan, S., (1997). "Development of Web-Based Educational Modules for Testing VHDL Models of Digital Systems" Thesis, Virginia Polytechnic Institute, and State University.
13. Lin, W., (2004). "A Case Study on Support Vector Machines Versus Artificial Neural Networks," Thesis, University of Pittsburgh.
14. Viñuela I. P., & Galván L. I., (2003). Artificial Neural Networks. A practical approach. Pearson Prentice Hall.
15. Salcedo Campos, F., (2003, May). Hidden Markov Models. Proc. IEEE. 1(3), 314–315.
16. Phung, S. L., Bouzerdoum, A., & Chai, D. (2005). Skin segmentation using color pixel classification: analysis and comparison. IEEE transactions on pattern analysis and machine intelligence, 27(1), 148-154.
17. Analysis and Comparison. IEEE sections on Pattern Analysis and Machine Intelligence, 27 (1), 148–154.
18. Basogian, X., (2008). Book Notes: Artificial Neural Networks and Applications. Retrieved on September 18, 2013, the Virtual Campus Website University.
19. Valvert, J. R., (2006). methods and techniques of face recognition in two-dimensional digital images. Graduate work unpublished, University of San Carlos, Colonia Santa Rosa, Guatemala.
20. Arguello, H., (2011). recognition Systems based on Facial Image. Journal Advances in Systems and Computer, 8 (3), 7–16.
21. Bracamonte, T. J., & Peter, L. S., (2007, November). Application of Kohonen Neural Network to Face Recognition. Paper presented at VI Peruanas Computing Week, Trujillo, Peru.
22. Rodriguez, E. G., & Sani, W. R., (2004). Design and implementation of a security system based on the recognition of human faces. Graduate work unpublished, National Polytechnic School, Quito, Ecuador.

23. Colonel, H. F., (2007). Face Recognition using Neural Networks. Graduate work unpublished, National Polytechnic School, Quito, Ecuador.

24. Goldstein, A. J., Harmon, L. D., & Lesk, A. B. (1971). Identification of human faces. Proceedings of the IEEE, 59(5), 748-760.

25. Rumelhart, D. E., & McClelland, J. L. (1986). Parallel distributed processing: explorations in the microstructure of cognition. volume 1. foundations.

26. Cottrell, G. W., & Munro, P. (1988, October). Principal components analysis of images via back propagation. In Visual Communications and Image Processing'88: Third in a Series (Vol. 1001, pp. 1070-1078). International Society for Optics and Photonics.

27. Hopfield, J. J., & Tank, D. W. (1985). "Neural" computation of decisions in optimization problems. Biological cybernetics, 52(3), 141-152.

28. Rosenblatt, F. (1958). The perceptron: a probabilistic model for information storage and organization in the brain. Psychological review, 65(6), 386.

29. Widrow, B., & Hoff, M. E. (1960). Adaptive switching circuits(No. TR-1553-1). Stanford Univ Ca Stanford Electronics Labs.

30. Rumelhart, D. E., Durbin, R., Golden, R., & Chauvin, Y. (1995). Backpropagation: The basic theory. Backpropagation: Theory, architectures and applications, 1-34.

INDEX

M

N

P

R

S